PONDERING
THE
GOODNESS
OF GOD

An Introductory Guide to
STILLNESS AND PRESENCE

VONDA FLUE

PONDERING THE GOODNESS OF GOD
An Introductory Guide To Stillness And Presence

Vonda Flue
hello@vondaflue.com

ISBN: 978-1-943342-53-2

Printed in the USA.
All rights reserved

Featuring Artwork by Tim Conner

Published by: Destined To Publish | Flossmoor, Illinois
www.DestinedToPublish.com

ACKNOWLEDGMENTS

First and foremost, I would like to give all the glory and honor to God, the object of my heart's affection and my mind's attention. I could write a book on that, and I probably will, but for now, I'll just say that this book declares my devotion to Him loud and clear.

I would like to thank my parents who gifted me with the love of reading. My mom read many books to me as a child. At a very young age she piqued my imagination with stories. When we go on vacations together, we both bring a book or two to read. We love a good adventure, but we also love a good book. My dad reads quite a lot as well. He has a very vivid imagination and would convey the wonder and awe of God when he would preach or teach. He piqued the contemplative side of me with those mental pictures and stories. Week Thirteen echoes one of his sermons, 'How Big Is Your God?' I would probably say that my dad's favorite books of the Bible are Isaiah and Ephesians. Isaiah tells us the magnitude of the God that loves us, Ephesians tells us we are seated right next to Him. Both books engage your imagination, which is the foundation for pondering.

I would also like to thank my cousin, Tim Conner, for allowing me to use his art in this book. I was mesmerized by the richness and serenity he conveyed in his art. The psalmist pondered God's creation and recreated it with words. Tim recreates it with pen and ink. Both ways lend themselves to pondering. Your gifting has greatly enriched this book. Thank you for providing the readers with a complimentary way to ponder.

ACKNOWLEDGMENTS

And lastly, this book would probably not be in your hands were it not for one statement from my close friend Tammy Hardey. On a dreary day, when I was quite sure that everyone else had already written everything that I wanted to write and much better than I could, she quicky replied, "But we haven't heard it from *you*." There were no rebuttals for such logic. She was right. We all have unique life experiences, which means that you will always have a unique story to tell (more on that subject is in the back of this book). Thanks for always believing in me. Thanks for letting me bounce ideas of you. That means more to me than you will ever know, and thanks for being an amazing and Godly friend!

DEDICATION

This book is dedicated, first and foremost to my mom. She recounts the story that before I could read, I would tell her if she missed a word when she read one of my books to me. Yes, that tells you that I was an attentive child, but it speaks volumes of a mother who would read a book repeatedly at a child's request. Those selfless acts birthed a love for words and a love for hearing a story told. I am sure God uses the same pathway to tell me stories today.

Thank you, mom, for the foundation and the cultivating for the love of words. I will be forever grateful for your investment into my life.

To my husband, Ken. Thank you for being my constant encourager and supporter no matter what I do. Thank you for speaking favor and success over my life and my writings. You patiently listen to me as I process out loud, usually for a much longer time than you wanted. You are an amazing man, and I am honored to walk along side of you.

TABLE OF CONTENTS

TABLE OF CONTENTS

INTRODUCTION

Sometimes in our busy, fast-paced world we rush through life. We don't stop and smell the roses. We don't sit and watch the sunset. We definitely don't ponder.

Ponder seems like such an archaic word. Maybe that's because I rarely hear it used, but it is one of my favorite words. Webster's dictionary defines *ponder* as "to weigh in the mind: appraise, to think about: reflect on." It goes on further to say, "to think or consider especially quietly, soberly, and deeply."

That's what I do every day with God. Whether I am in His word or out and about in His world, I weigh in the mind — I consider quietly and deeply. It is not a highly effective method in this fast-paced world. Pondering takes time, but God is worth my time. His goodness is a life-long study, and it never gets boring. Pondering stills my heart and my body thus allowing my mind and my cells to absorb His peace. His presence is what I desire. His presence brings peace. His presence brings all that I need.

You will notice in this book that I ponder on various subjects and in various ways. On the days when the sun is out and there is not a cloud in the sky, I ponder how such an amazing God could love someone like me. I ponder how this same God would clear His calendar to spend time with me. I ponder the goodness of God when it is smooth sailing, for it is the overwhelming goodness of God that draws me to sit with Him and stay a while. He is good, and it is good in His presence. The nearness of my God is for my good.

INTRODUCTION

"But as for me, the nearness of God is my good; I have made the Lord GOD my refuge, That I may tell of all Your works." Psalm 73:28 (NASB)

Nevertheless, not all my days are filled with peace. Sometimes life comes at me unexpectedly. Sometimes life throws a curve ball. Sometimes life stops me dead in my tracks. There will be a day on the other side of this life when the storm clouds will not roll in, but down here on planet Earth life lets in some very hard days, and very hard days can turn into really hard seasons. On those days, when the answers will not come, when the storms will not abate, when the end looks different than the God I know, I still ponder, for the nearness of my God is for my good in all seasons. Sitting with my Father is the solace to my soul. It is truly the only solace I know.

Yes, ponder is an archaic word, but it needs to be resurrected and inserted into our lives and language. It may be outdated, but I cannot let it go, for it has such a deep and rich meaning.

So, let us ponder on the word *ponder*. When trying to understand a word you may not be familiar with, look at the synonyms to give you a broader meaning of the word. Here are some synonyms for ponder from Webster's dictionary: "contemplate, deliberate, kick around, meditate, mull (over), question, ruminate, study, think (about, over), wrestle (with)." That last synonym is a good one. In the hard times, I "wrestle (with)" Him. When I am looking at what lies in front of me and I am struggling for resolution, clarification, or cessation, I still need to sit with my God. I call out. I cry out. I question. I may not understand, but if I know this one thing — the goodness of my God — then I can remain peaceful in the turmoil. This one thing keeps me from caving under the weight of the world.

Sometimes we grapple with the outcomes *and* the journey. Pondering asks the hard questions as it leans in to clear the cobwebs and unearth what was previously missed. This may sound like worry, but when the goodness of God is kept as the backdrop in the stories of our lives, pondering will carry a measure of settled peace, even in the struggle.

The struggle can be hard, but it should not lessen His goodness; it should draw us closer to Him. In Him is the goodness that we seek, the goodness that we need. My God is my "stronghold in the day of trouble." I will call out to Him no matter my circumstances.

"The LORD is good, A strength and stronghold in the day of trouble; He knows [He recognizes, cares for, and understands fully] those who take refuge and trust in Him." Nahum 1:7 (AMP)

You will hear both my wrestling and my praising loud and clear in the pages of this book, but there is nothing that does not end in the goodness of God.

"Give thanks to the LORD, for He is good; His faithful love endures forever." 1 Chronicles 16:34 (HCSB)

"They will overflow [like a fountain] when they speak of Your great and abundant goodness And will sing joyfully of Your righteousness." Psalm 145:7 (AMP)

How to get the most out of this book:

- **Section One:** Section One of this book is comprised of seven subjects with three weeks in each section and each week contains daily prompts. For some of you, completing all seven days will seem overwhelming but do not give the enemy a foothold in this area. Give yourself grace and ask God to help you grow exponentially in the midst of what you are able to do in this season. Although I believe that we should aim for completion, I do not want us to fall into legalism and subsequently make an idol out of perfection.

- **Section Two:** Section Two recaptures the seven subjects in the first section, but not in a weekly/daily format. Additionally, I provided quite a bit of support in Section One giving you a firm hold on my hand as you learn to ponder. However, in Section Two my desire was to lessen my hold and let you use the skills you just learned. Although support is still provided in this section, the prompts are a broader stroke in nature and both the reading and the prompts for each subject could probably be done in one sitting.

- **Daily Prompts:** Do not make the daily prompts a highly intellectual task. Simply read the passage each day and ask God to speak (James 1:5). You may not hear something at first and that is okay. Pondering is not a fast-paced experience. Wait for Him. He is faithful.

Let us talk a little more about the daily prompts. Since they are usually formulated in questions, let me release you right now to not write a single word if that hinders your engagement with God. You would be surprised how many people tell me they have solid, free-flowing thoughts in their head, but as soon as they pick up a pen, they cannot express themselves cohesively. You are fully aware of the communication style between you and God and if it is working, that is great. So, I release you, but I also challenge you—give Him room to expand your territories. We tend to get comfortable in an area if something is working, but we do not want to limit God to one mode of communication. Step out and doodle or jot down a word or a phrase. What He said must be important or He would not have taken the time to speak. You may think you will remember what He says, but I find that my memory fades with time so put it on paper somehow. Remember what they say, the palest ink is better than the best memory.

- **Creative Expression:** With that in mind, for those who hear God in other ways besides just words, there are blank pages in this book. I realize that I am a "words" person, hence this book in your hands, however, I want to give those who hear God in other ways the freedom to express themselves as well. The Bible is full of sights, sounds, visions, aromas and other ways that God used to communicate to His children. What He has done in the past is still available today, for He is the same God today, yesterday and forevermore. Feel free to use the blank areas for creative expression in ways like art, songwriting, or doodling. Our Father wants us to come as children so even if you end up with a childlike drawing, your Father would proudly display your artwork on His refrigerator if He had one. Be aware, also, that more of your senses may be stimulated when pondering because He fully engages in creativity when communicating. Therefore, be prepared to experience things in new ways. It may be just a matter of taking that first step of abandoning perfection so you and God can have a chuckle together over that attempt. If you do not feel creative in art, I encourage you to use the designated blank spaces to rewrite words or phrases that stand out to you. You could write them larger or in color. Even if you hear words, what does that look like in a picture? Go ahead and draw a little picture from time to time and your experience in pondering will be dramatically enhanced if your creative side is fully engaged. Allow the Lord the liberty to reveal Himself in any way He wants in your pondering time, and He may take you up on that offer.

Other helpful tips:

- **Write out James 1:5 on an index card or on a piece of paper to use as your bookmark.** You will use this scripture as a basis for your opening prayer time each day, so keep it handy for easy reference. The last six words in this verse, "…it will be given to him" is a promise based on the condition previously set: "ask." That's it. He simply says ask. That is an amazing promise from the God of the universe! Therefore, when you feel that you do not know how to answer a question or prompt in this book or you need an answer to the questions of life, remember those six simple words and cry out for what He promised. James 1:5 in expanded form is written below, but feel free to use whatever version you would like.

"If any of you lacks wisdom [to guide him through a decision or circumstance], he is to ask of [our benevolent] God, who gives to everyone generously and without rebuke or blame, and it will be given to him." (AMP)

- **Take time to ponder the pictures in this book.** They were placed there for just that purpose. Remember what they say, a picture is worth a thousand words. Let your eyes move over the picture and notice the beauty, the form, the colors and anything else that catches your eye. God can speak without using a single word.

- **While reading this book, take time to ponder (more on this in Section One).** If something stands out to you, feel free to close the book and spend time with God. Let Him expound on what He brought to your attention. Let us bring back the word *ponder* and use it with the One who desires it most. We need more than a passing glance at God. We need more than a drive-by scripture for the day and a head full of knowledge. We need more than a quick read to get us through the day. We need more of Him. We need to soak in His presence and let His goodness and wisdom seep into our cells and mind so that we can overflow on everyone we meet.

- **Be flexible and patient with yourself and me.** The passage to read each day will not be the same length, which means that your time to read may vary each day so be prepared but also do not worry. If you only have time for part of the reading, be at peace and glean from what you were able to read. God can speak to you through one word. Do what you can. He is not looking for a nice and tidy check-off list when spending time with Him. He is far more interested in the relationship than following the exact protocol laid out in this book.

- **You will be asked numerous times in this book to reread something.** We repeat an action to lean into the deeper meaning and revelation. Reading something repeatedly is a form of ponder. You may have missed something the first time or He may highlight something new when you read it again.

- **I have with great intention set the pace for this book. It should be a pace that allows for pondering.** If you do not know what that pace looks like, it would probably be the pace an average person would leisurely walk while gazing at their surroundings, occasionally stopping to examine something more closely or to pausing to rest. That, my friend, is a great pace to walk with the One who lives outside of time. He is not in a hurry. He is not wearing a wristwatch. He is willing to walk with you. With that in mind, let us learn more about pondering.

PRACTICING THE PONDER

Let's do a quick pondering activity using just two scriptures from the book of Jonah. If are not familiar with this story, pause and go read the four short chapters of this amazing book. The gist of the story is that God called Jonah to go one way and Jonah went the other way. Yes, He *intentionally* purchased passage on a boat going in the completely opposite direction. He paid good money to *deliberately* disobey and then promptly went below the deck to sleep. God, on the other hand, did not allow Jonah to sleep off his bad decision.

> *"Then the LORD sent a great wind on the sea, and such a violent storm arose that the ship threatened to break up." Jonah 1:4 (NLT)*

The rest of the story goes like this: the sailors tossed their cargo overboard to lighten the load but to no avail. Then they figured out that Jonah was running from the Lord, who was also the same God who made everything, including the sea that had this violent storm. After scolding him for bringing this upon them, he gave them the solution—toss him overboard, but they cared about his life and tried rowing against the storm instead. When they realized that they could not do anything to save their lives or Jonah's life, they went through with the strange solution to end a storm:

Then the sailors picked Jonah up and threw him into the raging sea, and the storm stopped at once!" Jonah 1:15 (NLT)

Let us ponder these verses for a moment. Set your timer for two minutes and silence your phone as well to prevent any distractions so that you remain focused on the text for the full two minutes.

Read both verses again and imagine yourself as one of the sailors. What it would be like to be in a raging storm that had you terrified of losing everything including your life? Notice that the text does not say that the storm progressively "calmed down." It says that it "*stopped at once.*" What would your reaction be to an instant cessation of a terrifying storm? What would your thoughts be as you looked out across a clear sky while you were still soaking wet from the waves that were crashing against the boat *literally* just one second prior? What would you be thinking as you are still clutching the railing, gasping for breath, and spitting water out of your mouth but you are on a perfectly serene boat? That was what I was envisioning and thinking about when I was listening to my husband talk about the story of Jonah. I did not plan to ponder but that scene and those thoughts were so vivid. Did you think of anything else? Read those verses one more time before we go on and see if God reveals anything else to you.

That is how you ponder. It really was not that difficult, was it? I wanted you to see that pondering does not need to be a lengthy process or a massive undertaking. You just need to be able to spend any amount of time on the same thing to look, listen, perceive, or wait. In this book, we do those things by returning to the same subject matter repeatedly. You will read my pondering questions to see what pondering really looks like.

Let me go ahead and give you a few practical and simple tips for pondering before we wrap up the Jonah activity.

- **First, you will need devoted time.** I know life is busy and it seems like a hundred requests come your way by the minute, but there must be a deliberate stepping out of the rat race, even if it only for a few minutes. Pondering does not need to be a prolonged process, but it does need to be a devoted process.

- **Secondly, silence your phone**. Go ahead and turn it over also so the auditory and visual notifications do not vie for your attention either. It is extremely advantageous if you can ponder something for an extended period of time. For example, if you were contemplating purchasing a precious stone or a rare find, you would want to inspect it. You would take the time to turn it in various ways so you could see it from every angle possible in case there are flaws or to appreciate the beauty. An expensive purchase is worth the time. The treasures you will unearth in pondering will most definitely be worth your time.

- **Next, "switch gears."**

  ○ When we are running in the fast lane, it can be difficult to downshift to a slower pace. Putting the brakes on our "what if" thoughts and quieting our body can be a hard transition sometimes. It's okay to take an extra step or two to make this transition. You may want to put on worship music, as the Bible says that He inhabits the praises of His people. You could also read a passage of scripture that declares His unfailing love for His children or use you could use your own words to thank Him that He has stated to be faithful to come if we invite Him.

  ○ If you are anything like me and your brain is always active, you may need to do a few other things to "switch gears." You might want to have a pen and paper with you to "brain dump." If you can write down all the things you need to remember or need to do, then you could disengage a little easier. If you more thoughts come up, don't fret; just grab the pen and quickly jot it down and return to your time with Him.

- **Lastly, wait.** Your time of ponder could be as little as a few minutes or could be as long as a day or two. Listen to the nudging of the spirit that is communicating to you to wait and stay for a minute; don't go anywhere. If you don't feel like He says or shows you anything right away, that's okay. You will grow at this skill, and you will find His rhythm so you will be able to effortlessly move in and out of pondering at any time of the day. Who knows, maybe pondering will become the norm, and chaotic will not find a place to lay its head. The enemy wants you busy. God wants you to 'be still and know.'

Let's conclude the pondering activity about the sailors and see if we learned anything valuable. As I personally pondered this part of the story, I would have been without words when the storm "stopped at once." I would not have had the capacity to explain what just happened, even to my massively drenched, rail-clutching, water-spitting fellow sailors. I would have been awestruck. I would have been speechless. I would have had no other choice but to glorify the God that Jonah served, and that is exactly what happened:

> *"The sailors were awestruck by the LORD's great power, and they offered him a sacrifice and vowed to serve him." Jonah 1:16 (NLT)*

Those sailors did not have a Bible to study. David did not have a Bible like we have today to study God either. He simply did what the sailors did – he noticed God clearly through what was in front of him.

> *"The heavens are telling of the glory of God; And their expanse is declaring the work of His hands." Psalm 19:1 (NLT)*

> *"For ever since the world was created, people have seen the earth and sky. Through everything God made, they can clearly see his invisible qualities—his eternal power and divine nature. So they have no excuse for not knowing God." Romans 1:20 (NLT)*

We can learn about God by studying God's word, but we also can learn about Him by sitting with the text and pondering. Pondering 101 may not be a course you can take in seminary, but I am positive that He wrote a book that everyone can understand if we slow down, spend time with Him and just read. God is so good to have made it that simple.

Now, let me be clear, there are days when I don't feel like I understand what I read so I find a commentary or two to help me better understand, yet so many times He meets me *where I am*. Which means that He speaks through the words I *do understand*. Why wouldn't He be that good? Let's make pondering the goodness of God a lifelong journey.

PEACE

Let the peace of Christ [the inner calm of one who walks daily with Him] be the controlling factor in your hearts [deciding and settling questions that arise]. To this peace indeed you were called as members in one body [of believers]. And be thankful [to God always].

Colossians 3:15 (AMP)

WEEK ONE
PEACEFUL IN THE CHAOS

I want to be wise and not fearful in my decisions; therefore, I will relentlessly pursue what I am supposed to pursue, the peace of God and the God of peace.

Peace comes from knowing God. Knowing God allows you to know that although chaos and calamity may come, God has never left His throne.

I am not immune to diseases nor disasters, but I am in control of my mind's attention and my heart's affection.

May I be seen as peaceful in the chaos.

May I be seen as His.

Personal testimony: For years I had lived with a spirit of fear. One day, I drew a line in the sand. I said, 'No more.' The change was immediate in many ways. My kidney stopped hurting, my muscle aches decreased, my breathing became calmer, and I simply felt better emotionally, spiritually, and physically. Although fear has crept back in other, sometimes more subtle forms (Satan never concedes to a loss), I recognize it and deal with it.

DAILY TIME WITH GOD:

DAY 1:

➢ Take a moment to pray. Tell God that you know He is willing to speak, but you want to be willing to hear what He says to you today and every day. (James 1:5)

➢ Read the devotion again.

➢ What does it take to be wise in your decisions?

_____

_____

_____

_____

_____

➢ Does that mean that you will be perfect in your decisions? What does it look like to God when you make a mistake? (Make sure you are thinking of what God would think, not what you would think).

_____

_____

_____

_____

_____

DAY 2:

➢ Take a moment to pray. Use James 1:5 as your guide to ask Him to speak. Take a moment to listen.

➢ Read the devotion again as this will help you ponder.

➢ "…the peace of God and the God of peace." Everyone wants the peace of God; however, it is essential to know the God of peace before you can experience the peace of God, as my dad so clearly explained one day. Ponder this for a moment.

➢ Reflect and express what God just revealed to you.

_____

_____

_____

_____

_____

_____

DAY 3:

➤ Take a moment to pray then read the devotion again.
Ponder this quote from the devotion: "Peace come from knowing God. Knowing God allows you to know that chaos and calamity may come, but God has never left His throne." There must be a settled, determined state of mind that God is in control, i.e. He has never left His throne. What does it look like to you that God has never left His throne?

_____

_____

_____

_____

_____

➤ Reflect and express what God is saying to you.

_____

_____

_____

_____

DAY 4:

➤ Take a moment to pray. Thank Him for the peace that He brings to your life.
➤ Read the devotion again.

➤ "…chaos and calamity may come…" Jesus said in John 16:33, "I have told you all this so that you may have peace in me. Here on earth you will have many trials and sorrows. But take heart, because I have overcome the world." (NLT) Ponder the fact that Jesus knows about the chaos and calamity here on this earth, but He has overcome the world. What does that mean, practically, to you in your everyday life?

_____

_____

_____

_____

➤ Reflect and express what God just revealed to you.

_____

_____

_____

_____

DAY 5:

➤ Begin your time with prayer using James 1:5 as your guide then read the devotion again.
➤ "I am not immune to diseases nor disasters, but I am in control of my mind's attention and my heart's affection." How do you take control of your mind's attention? How do you take control of your heart's affection? How do you practically live out both when disease and disasters come?

_____

_____

_____

_____

_____

➤ Reflect and express what God just revealed to you.

_____

_____

_____

_____

DAY 6

➤ Take a little time to pray before you begin, then read the devotion again.
➤ Read the devotion again.
➤ "May I be seen as peaceful in the chaos. May I be seen as His." Christians are called to be different. We are not to look like the world. The world does not have an anchor when chaos or calamity comes. Ponder the recent events of your life that may have been less than what you would have wanted or expected. Were you able to react differently than a person who does not have Christ as their anchor and hope? Were you able to be peaceful in the situation? What is God saying to you right now?

_____

_____

_____

_____

DAY 7:

➤ Take a moment to pray. Tell God that you know He is willing to speak, but you want to be willing to hear what He says to you today and every day. (James 1:5)
➤ Read the devotion again.

➢ Read Days 1-6 again in their entirety.

➢ Reflect on the past days and express below what God has revealed using the lines or the blank space.

_____

_____

_____

_____

_____

Creative Expressions

BE STILL AND KNOW – PART ONE

"Be still, and know that I am God..." Psalm 46:10 (ESV)

Getting to know God is so exciting. Psalm 46:10 says that we can know God, but it connects knowing with stillness. Stillness is not a popular word in our American society. It is not something we invite our friends over to talk about while sipping tea. Stillness is not something most people want to talk about at all much less engage in. Stillness seems to cut against the fabric of our being as productive humans.

Yet stillness is what God is asking for. When I talk about this quiet, still time that we are called to have with the Lord, I frequently hear this response, "I don't know how to just sit and do nothing. How do you do that?" Stillness gets compared to boredom, and if all you do is sit and do nothing, that would be pretty boring, but this verse does not tell you to sit and do nothing.

The inability to be still is painfully evident in those who have experienced trauma. As an occupational therapist who works with traumatized individuals, I see this unfortunate side effect of trauma. These individuals do not want to be caught by surprise, so they are always on guard. It appears to be a good solution initially, but the body cannot sustain the constant hyper-vigilance needed to analyze all incoming data to assess whether they are safe. A major problem occurs when they stop moving; the body goes in the complete opposite direction to recover the resources they are doling out to survive and they begin to shut down. Not long after stillness occurs, the eyes start blinking slower, they stare off into space, the yawning begins, and they can be asleep within minutes if no intervention occurs.

My goal is to teach them how to reduce high stress behaviors and mindset, but also to teach them that they can be still and not go to sleep. Experience is the best teacher, so we repeatedly practice activities to help them learn this. I let them choose a place to relax, then I play a couple of songs. When I notice that their body is beginning to shut down, I may ask a question or two to help them realize what is happening. During this simple activity they begin to learn how to still their body while allowing their mind to remain peacefully aware or lightly engaged in the world around them. The goal is rest in conscious repose.

Just looking around, listening to music or engaging in a short conversation can keep them from falling asleep as their mind disengages from purposeful survival mode. Once the body experiences the ability to stop moving without falling asleep, they can enjoy such events as time with family or friends around the campfire or just sitting and talking after an evening meal.

Your mind can be focused on Him and peacefully aware of the world around you at the same time. Your stillness allows the presence of God to be felt more tangibly. Your stillness allows the words of God to be heard more clearly. He gave the command to 'be still' because He knew that our busy cells would need to learn to quiet themselves.

Another barrier to being still before God is a wandering mind. People start off intending to focus on God, but the to-do list pulls their mind's attention away from the Father. Our minds are wired to think, and when we try to think of nothing, something will come up. It is a little uncanny how many to-do lists come up when the focus is supposed to be on God. Our enemy is always working to sabotage our time with the Father. Between our wandering minds, the to-do list or sleepiness, we can quickly feel discouraged that the act of being still before God can be attained.

Your thoughts are the intangible world where you and the Creator of the universe meet. Give that thought life to God who is the author of your thought life. He knows what to do with it. Think about it this way, boredom comes when you focus on what you cannot do; inspiration comes when you focus on what you can do. True inspiration comes when you focus on what you can do in conjunction with the One who can do all things.

God knew we would need time of stillness to "declutter and clean out" our minds of our feeble attempts at solutions, so He commanded us to be still and find rest for our souls. The sabbath was created with the same concept in mind. Do you realize that by your nonstop actions, you are telling Him that what He has provided is not enough? Do you refuse the gift of peace

He offers? Do you take the time to declutter and refill with His solutions? Do you take the time at all?

"Be still and know that I am God."

I love to have my times of stillness with God in the mornings. The house is still slumbering, and there is a sacred silence awaiting me. I know that God is in that space, and I want to be in that space with Him. I can take away its sacredness by filling it with the things of this life, or I can refuse the distractions and soak in His presence. During my time with Him, I hear Him. A thought comes into my head as I am pondering life or reading His word. He speaks so eloquently in the stillness, and suddenly I see things from a totally different perspective. My body offers no distractions. My cells are quiet, waiting for their Masters' next words. My mind is attentive to only Him. This is where hope is born. My hope is in the Lord.

"Why are you cast down, O my soul, and why are you in turmoil within me? Hope in God; for I shall again praise him, my salvation and my God." Psalm 42:11 (ESV)

Do not let the enemy steal your time with God. Do not listen to the enemy when he says that quiet time is boring. He is called the father of lies for a reason. Do not listen to him when he tells you that you do not know how to be still, for God created the Sabbath for that very reason. You were created for relationship, and the most important relationship of all is with your loving Heavenly Father. Busyness creates a relationship with chaos, and chaos is not from God.

"Be still and know that I am God."

DAILY TIME WITH GOD:

DAY 1:

➤ Take a moment to pray. Tell God that you know He is willing to speak, but you want to be willing to hear what He says to you today and every day. (James 1:5)
➤ Read the devotion again.
➤ What happens when you finally stop moving? Do you watch television? Do you read? Do you work puzzles? Do you keep doing something, so you do not fall asleep? Do you think of the things you need to do?

_____

_____

_____

_____

_____

➤ We do know that we can hear God anywhere and at any time, so why do you think the passage connects being still and knowledge?

_____

_____

_____

_____

_____

➤ Reflect. If you already know how to be still before Him, thank Him for giving you that knowledge and pray that you are a faithful doer of what you know. If you do not know how to be still before Him, then pray and ask Him to create a desire and hunger to learn more and then to be a faithful doer of what you learn.

_____

_____

_____

_____

_____

DAY 2:

➤ Take a moment to pray using James 1:5 as your guide then read the devotion again.

➤ Take a moment to pay attention to your cells. Are they excessively busy with worry or fear? Are the cells in your lungs being directed to create shallow, chest-level breaths or deep peaceful, relaxing breaths that move into your core? Are the cells in your muscles tight and hurting, or are they able to move when needed and rest when not needed? You get the point. Have you trained your cells to be excessively busy, or do they know how to obey the command to be still?

➤ Reflect and express what God just revealed to you.

_____

_____

_____

_____

_____

DAY 3:

➤ Take a moment to pray then read the devotion again.

➤ What does this mean to you: "God is the author of your imagination. Your imagination is the intangible world where you and the Creator of the universe meet."

_____

_____

_____

_____

➤ Take a moment and ponder what you use your imagination for. Is it an undefiled channel through which you can hear?

_____

_____

_____

_____

_____

➤ Reflect and express what God just revealed to you.

_____

_____

_____

_____

_____

DAY 4:

➤ Take a moment to pray. Tell God that you know He is willing to speak, but you want to be willing to hear what He says to you today and every day. (James 1:5)
➤ Read the devotion again.
➤ "Do you realize that by your non-stop actions, you are telling Him that what He has provided is not enough? Do you refuse the gift of peace He offers? Do you take the time to declutter and refill with His solutions? Do you take the time at all?"
➤ Reflect and express what God just revealed to you.

_____

_____

_____

_____

_____

DAY 5:

➤ Don't forget to pray before you begin.
➤ Read the devotion again.
➤ When do you meet with Him? In the morning? In the evening? What makes that time so special?

_____

_____

_____

_____

_____

➢ Write out a prayer for strength to always keep that time sacred (set apart) for you to meet with Him. Include a clause if that time is taken away, while on vacation. For example, how do you want Him to call you back to Him? He wants to go on vacation with us!

_____

_____

_____

_____

_____

DAY 6

➢ Take a moment to pray. Tell God that you know He is willing to speak, but you want to be willing to hear what He says to you today and every day. (James 1:5)

➢ Read the devotion again.

➢ Have you ever thought about being still like this: "My body offers no distractions. My cells are quiet, waiting for their Masters' next words. My mind is attentive to only Him. This is where hope is born. My hope is in the Lord."

➢ Write out a prayer confessing the times you did not control your body so you could connect with Him the way He has directed. (Remember, that is not the only way we connect and hear Him, but it is a great way and a commanded way).

_____

_____

_____

_____

Day 7:

➢ Take a moment to pray and just be still before Him for a moment.

➢ Read the devotion again.

➢ Read Days 1-6 again in their entirety.

➢ Reflect on the past days and express below what God has revealed to you.

_____

_____

_____

_____

_____

Creative Expressions

WEEK THREE

Be Still And Know – Part 2

Last week we talked about being still before the Lord, but there is another way to look at it. God did not *ask* us to be still and know that He is God, He *commanded* it. I do not think that He would have given us this commandment if it were not possible.

Why don't you take a few minutes to assess your heart, not as a judgmental shame-based tactic, but as an honest evaluation of your heart's affections? We *can* be still. We can do it for long periods of time, such as during church, during a recital or play, or a two-hour movie. We may wiggle, but for the most part we quiet our bodies and engage in what is in front of us. You *can* do it. You have probably done it more times than you realize.

Ask God to show you what is different when you sit still for other activities like a recital or a movie versus when you sit still before Him. For example, when the pastor at church or the plot of a movie is leading our minds, we focus on something tangible in front of us. However, when you sit with God, there may not be anything in front of you except your Bible; therefore, you must control the direction of your thoughts. Many people say that this is the biggest struggle. Ask Him why you struggle with that control. Remember, James 1:5 says that if we ask, He will reply.

Are there too many things awaiting our attention on that to-do list? Ask God what needs pruning. Ask Him to show you where change can happen so life doesn't crowd into every corner of your mind. He already knows these things. He knows right where you could use

some pruning. Also, ask Him to remind you of the sweetness of His company all day long so that 'the things of earth will grow strangely dim in the light of His glory and grace'.[1] Long for His presence as a deer pants for water. Sometimes it is not as much about stopping an action as it is replacing an action with a more desirable action.

Spend time with the most important person you will ever get a chance to spend time with today and every day.

Soak in His goodness so you will be able to pour out that same goodness on a hurting and fearful world today and every day.

Sit at His feet so that you can know what is pure, holy, and right so you can order yourself and your day accordingly, today and every day.

Being still before Him changes you so that you are made new in the old world that you are still a part of.

Being still before Him is the best action one can take for the day.

Are you being still before the Lord?

Personal Testimony: I am working on deliberately trying to be still before Him. God and I talk ALL day long. I am thankful that He is a good listener because I can talk quite a bit; however, I desperately need time to be still and hear Him. That is more important than making my requests incessantly known because my Father knows I have need of these things. The enemy works so hard to steal that sweet, intimate, satisfying time with Him.

I need that time, or I slowly drift. If a ship is just one degree off when crossing the ocean, it can end up at a vastly different place.[2] Many of us, including myself, usually do not seem to notice how far that we have drifted until we are physically or emotionally in a vastly different place.

DAILY TIME WITH GOD:

DAY 1:

➤ Take a moment to pray. Tell God that you know He is willing to speak, but you want to be willing to hear what He says to you today and every day. (James 1:5)
➤ Read the devotion again.

➢ What does it mean to you to be still before the Lord? Is it a physical posture or spiritual mindset, or both? What do you do with your emotions?

_____

_____

_____

_____

_____

➢ Reflect and express what God just revealed to you.

_____

_____

_____

_____

_____

DAY 2:

➢ Be still for a moment and pray.
➢ Read the devotion again.
➢ Why would our hearts be involved in being still before the Lord? Could it be that our affection for the things of the Spirit is not as strong as our affections for the duties of the day? Ponder which affections are stronger and why?

_____

_____

_____

_____

_____

➢ Reflect and express what God just revealed to you.

_____

_____

_____

_____

_____

DAY 3:

➢ Take a moment to pray. It's worth the time to invite Him to come.
➢ Read the devotion again.
➢ Notice that I added this comment when I recommended that you take an assessment of your heart, "Not as a judgmental shame-based tactic, but as an honest evaluation of your heart's affections." I added it because we all tend to fall into the trap of the enemy to shame ourselves over our shortcomings. We continue to live under condemnation for our sins instead of in the power of God's words, "there is no condemnation for those who are in Christ Jesus." Romans 8:1 (NIV)

_____

_____

_____

_____

_____

➢ Reflect and express what God is saying to you.

_____

_____

_____

_____

_____

Day 4:

➢ Take a moment to pray using James 1:5 as your guide.

➢ Read the devotion again.

➢ Once you have taken an inventory of your heart's affections, then you can "ask God to show you what needs pruning." When your hands are full of your own things, it is much more difficult to receive what He has for you during your time with Him.

_____

_____

_____

_____

_____

➢ Reflect and express what God just revealed to you.

_____

_____

_____

_____

_____

Day 5:

➢ Take a moment to pray then read the devotion again.

➢ Why would you need Him to remind you of the sweetness of His company? Shouldn't our memory of it be sufficient? Oh, how quickly our to-do list 'runneth over' and time with Him seems out of reach. He will gently remind you of your time with Him, but remember, His "language" is different than ours. He may remind you with words, but He is also fond of using such things as a picture, a flower, a dream, or a feeling of indescribable peace. Allow Him to speak to You in whatever way He wants. He will find the perfect way to remind you of your need for time with Him. Follow Him at His first invitation. "Spend time with the most important person you will ever get a chance to be with right now."

➢ Reflect and express what God just revealed to you.

_____

_____

_____

_____

_____

DAY 6:

➢ Take a moment to pray. Tell God that you know He is willing to speak, but you want to be willing to hear what He says to you today and every day. (James 1:5)

➢ Read the devotion again.

➢ We need to spend time with Him for ourselves "so that we can know what is pure, holy and right so that we can order ourselves and our day accordingly," but this life is not all about ourselves. We will be called upon at some point in our day to help others, maybe multiple times a day. The only way you can "pour that same goodness out on a hurting and fearful world today is to sit at His feet, to be still before Him."

➢ Reflect and express what God just revealed to you.

_____

_____

_____

_____

_____

Day 7:

➢ Take a moment to pray. Remember to thank Him.

➢ Read the devotion again.

➢ Read Days 1-6 again in their entirety.

➢ Reflect on the past days and express below what God has revealed to you.

_____

_____

_____

_____

_____

Creative Expressions

THE VALUE OF PONDERING –
THE VALUE OF RELATIONSHIP

. . . .

I would like to spend a quick moment expounding on the value of pondering. For me, this book was born out of time with God as I did not set out years ago to write a book. I just began to spend unhurried time with my heavenly Father. (I will use the phrase "unhurried time" in this book because it was so pivotal to my relationship with Him). During that "unhurried time," He began to speak; He began to download stories. Pondering grew out of time with Him. I pondered *why* the God of the universe would choose to speak to me, but I also spent quite a bit of time pondering *what* He said to me.

I want to hear Him more. I believe you do as well. Pondering can improve the growth, capacity, and the depth of your relationship with God to the point where, when He wants to give you something, it comes like a download all at once because you've already prepared the ground for that direct download communication. To say that simply, when you sit and ponder, you are more available for a download.

In all honesty, I value pondering because I value Him. Pondering allows me to move past the list I bring or even past the answers He has, for it is relationship that He values. Pondering allows me to feel His presence, to hear His heartbeat, and to soak in His peace. Pondering gives me a backstage glimpse at the most amazing person who loves me more than I can imagine. In a nutshell, I value pondering because I value my relationship with the Father. This book was born out of that deep desire to know Him more. I trust that you want that as well.

SURRENDER

Now therefore, if you will indeed obey my voice and keep my covenant, you shall be my treasured possession among all peoples, for all the earth is mine; and you shall be to me a kingdom of priests and a holy nation.'

Exodus 19:5-6 (ESV)

Glimpses Of God

"Sometimes when you give up, God shows up." – Vonda Flue

I have learned so much in this season of my life.

Each season I go through, I get a glimpse of different aspects of God.
Each season I go through, I get a glimpse of different aspects of me.

Wisdom.
Grace.
Surrender.
Prayer.
Love.
Patience.

The faithfulness of God.
The longsuffering of God.
The beckoning of God.
The chastisement of God.

Reaping and sowing.
Forgiveness.

Silence.
Trust.

Standards.
Perseverance.
Integrity.
Vulnerability.

But God, who is rich in mercy.
The nearness of my God is my good.
My God shall supply all your needs.

My God.
My Father.
My refuge.
My guide.
My shelter.

DAILY TIME WITH GOD:

DAY 1:

➢ Take a moment to pray. Tell God that you know He is willing to speak, but you want to be willing to hear what He says to you today and every day. (James 1:5)
➢ Read the devotion again.
➢ Giving up does not mean the same thing in the physical world as it does in the spiritual world. In the physical world, I give up when I feel defeated and powerless. In the spiritual world, giving up means I stop using my power and let God be God.
➢ With that in mind, what does this statement mean to you?
"Sometimes when you give up, God shows up."

_____

_____

_____

_____

_____

DAY 2:

- ➤ Take a moment to pray. You know He is listening to His child, so take the time to be with Him then read the devotion again.
- ➤ Read this list:
  - ◦ Wisdom.
  - ◦ Grace.
  - ◦ Surrender.
  - ◦ Prayer.
  - ◦ Love.
  - ◦ Patience.
- ➤ In which of the above words do you want to grow the most in this season? Why?

_____

_____

_____

_____

_____

DAY 3:

- ➤ Take a moment to pray, then read the devotion again. Remember, reading something over and over again is a form of ponder.
- ➤ What have you learned in this season of life about:
  - ◦ the faithfulness of God?
  - ◦ the longsuffering of God during this season of life?
  - ◦ the beckoning of God during this season of life?
  - ◦ The chastisement of God during this season of life?

_____

_____

_____

_____

DAY 4:

➤ Take a moment to pray. Tell God that you know He is willing to speak, but you want to be willing to hear what He says to you today and every day. (James 1:5)

➤ Read the devotion again.

➤ Take a moment to read each words below. God may speak to you about one. Write what He is saying. Then turn those words into a prayer below. You don't have to use all the words but write what He is saying to you.

   ○ Reaping and sowing.
   ○ Forgiveness.
   ○ Silence.
   ○ Trust.
   ○ Standards.
   ○ Perseverance.
   ○ Integrity.
   ○ Vulnerability.

_____

_____

_____

_____

_____

DAY 5:

➤ Take a few moments to pray, then read the devotion again.

➤ Read this list:

   ○ My God.
   ○ My Father.
   ○ My refuge.
   ○ My guide.
   ○ My shelter.

➢ Which of the statements above resonate with you during this season? Why? Write out a prayer to thank Him for being that for you during this season.

_____

_____

_____

_____

_____

DAY 6

➢ Pray before you begin as you have done each day.
➢ Read the devotion again.
➢ What have you learned about yourself during this season? What has God shown you about you?

_____

_____

_____

_____

_____

DAY 7:

➢ Take a moment to pray. Tell God that you know He is willing to speak, but you want to be willing to hear what He says to you today and every day. (James 1:5)
➢ Read the devotion again.
➢ Read Days 1-6 again in their entirety.
➢ Reflect on the past days and express below what God has revealed to you.

_____

_____

_____

_____

Creative Expressions

A DEFEATED RESPONSE

"I need more hours in the day."

I have said that phrase so many times in my life. When my children were young, it was my constant mantra. As a parent, there was always another task to do and there never seemed to be enough hours in the day.

Have you ever said those words? I think we all have. Maybe a better question is 'How many times have you said those words?' Do you find yourself still saying those words? That long to-do list will make you feel over-burdened and overwhelmed. One day, I offered this solution, "I need more hours in the day!"

Do you feel that more hours in a day would allow you to get to the end of that to-do list and sleep in peace? I don't think that solution would solve the problem because we would probably fill the empty spaces with more activity. Humans try to cram as much as they can into one time slot, one shopping trip, one vacation, etc. When people say they have to come home to rest after vacation, our society must breed into us the mindset of 'full to the brim.' Our society also has a 'more is better' mindset. Have you ever moved into a bigger house? When you walked in, you thought to yourself I will never be able to fill up all these rooms and all these cabinets. Yet, in just a few short years, the cabinets and rooms are overflowing, and the vehicles sit in the driveway while the abundance of stuff gets shaded in the garage. Don't worry, I have been there as well. Often, when people retire, they have busier schedules than they ever did when they were working a full-time job. Whatever it is, we tend to fill empty spaces, so I am not sure our calendars would fare any better with more hours in a day.

Longing for more hours in a day is probably a defeated response to the overwhelm we feel when our to-do list is longer than our 24-hour day. But take a moment and think about creation. God designed a 24-hour day. Not a 25- nor a 28-hour day, but a day consisting specifically of twenty-four hours. His response to His created 24-hour day was completely different than ours. Let's look at His response in scripture.

"And God said, "Let there be light," and there was light. And God saw that the light was good. And God separated the light from the darkness. God called the light Day, and the darkness he called Night. And there was evening and there was morning, the first day." *Genesis 1:3-5 (ESV)*

*"And God said, "Let there be lights in the expanse of the heavens to separate the day from the night. And let them be for signs and for seasons and for days and years, and let them be lights in the expanse of the heavens to give light upon the earth." And it was so. And God made the two great lights—the greater light to rule the day and the lesser light to rule the night—and the stars. And God set them in the expanse of the heavens to give light on the earth, to rule over the day and over the night, and to separate the light from the darkness. **And God saw that it was good.**"* *Genesis 1: 14-18 (ESV) (emphasis mine).*

When God created a 24-hour day, He said it was good. Twenty-four good hours. Ponder for a moment on a 24-hour day that is good. What would that look like? What would you feel like? What would you get accomplished? A good 24-hour day would be just enough hours to get in a good day's work and then, in sweet contentment, enjoy a good night of His restorative, rejuvenating sleep, waking refreshed for another good day.

The only way to get out of the overwhelm you feel when your to-do list is longer than your 24-hour day, is to allow Him to guide your to-do list. Instead of telling God that He was wrong for giving only 24 hours in a day, ask Him to guide your activities through His plans each minute of the 24 hours that He has given to us. Success is then guaranteed.

Let's look at Jesus. He had the same 24-hours in each day, and even He did not have time to do everything that the world clamored at Him to do. When Jesus left this earth, there were still people who were unsaved, unhealed, and demonized, yet He successfully completed the mission God sent Him to do. Jesus did only what the Father told Him to do each day. Jesus was successful during His earthly life with 24-hour days. I would say that success is measured differently in the kingdom. Success is not getting all your to-do list done in 24 hours. Success is doing what the Father tells you to do in the twenty-four hours He has given.

DAILY TIME WITH GOD:

DAY 1:

➢ Take a moment to pray. Tell God that you know He is willing to speak, but you want to be willing to hear what He says to you today and every day. (James 1:5)

➢ Read the devotion again.

➢ Genesis 1:1 is listed below with an emphasis on a different word or phrase each time. Read each line out loud.

> "**IN** the beginning God created the heavens and the earth."
>
> "In **THE BEGINNING** God created the heavens and the earth."
>
> "In the beginning **GOD** created the heavens and the earth."
>
> "In the beginning God **CREATED** the heavens and the earth."
>
> "In the beginning God created **THE HEAVENS** and the earth."
>
> "In the beginning God created the heavens **AND THE EARTH**."

➢ In Genesis 1:3-5 God recorded the first day, "And God said, "Let there be light," and there was light. And God saw that the light was good. And God separated the light from the darkness. God called the light Day, and the darkness he called Night. And there was evening and there was morning, the first day." We often think of God creating the day, but God created the darkness as well. God separated the light and the darkness. He must have had plans for the darkness (i.e. sleep, rest, restoration…).

➢ Reflect and express below what God just revealed to you about Him creating everything, even a 24-hour day which includes darkness:

_____

_____

_____

_____

DAY 2:

➤ Take a moment to pray. Just sit for a moment longer and be still, then read the devotion again.

➤ How often do you say or feel like you need more hours in a day? What are your thoughts about that now?

➤ Reflect and express below what God just showed you:

_____

_____

_____

_____

_____

DAY 3:

➤ Take a moment to pray. Hopefully, praying before you read is becoming more routine now that we have been practicing it for a while.

➤ Read the devotion again.

➤ Do you ever weave a request in your prayers for God to help you see or hear exactly what He wants you to do today?

➤ Do you ever weave a request in your prayers for God to help you see what He wants you to do every minute of the day?

➤ What are your thoughts about that now?

➤ Reflect and express below what God just showed you:

_____

_____

_____

_____

_____

DAY 4:

➤ Take a moment to pray. Tell God that you know He is willing to speak, but you want to be willing to hear what He says to you today and every day. (James 1:5)

➤ Read the devotion again.

➤ "Worthy are You, our Lord and our God, to receive glory and honor and power; for You created all things, and because of Your will they existed, and were created." Revelation 4:11 (NASB)

➤ Spend time thanking Him for creating all things.

➤ Spend time giving Him glory and honor for creating a 24-hour day.

➤ Ponder for a moment on a 24-hour day that is good. Twenty-four good hours. What would that look like?

➤ What are your thoughts about a 24-hour day now?

➤ Reflect and express below what God just showed you:

_____

_____

_____

_____

_____

DAY 5:

➤ Take a moment to pray, then read the devotion again.

➤ "So Jesus said to them, "Truly, truly, I say to you, the Son can do nothing of his own accord, but only what he sees the Father doing. For whatever the Father does, that the Son does likewise" John 5:18-20 (ESV)

➤ What are your thoughts about what Jesus said that he could and could not do?

➤ How does that relate to your 24-hour day?

➤ Reflect and express below what God just showed you:

_____

_____

_____

DAY 6:

➤ Take a moment to pray. Tell God that you know He is willing to speak, but you want to be willing to hear what He says to you today and every day. (James 1:5)

➤ Read the devotion again.

➤ "Let us fix our eyes on Jesus, the author and perfecter of our faith, who for the joy set before Him endured the cross, scorning its shame, and sat down at the right hand of the throne of God." Hebrews 12:2 (BSB)

➤ Jesus did only what the Father told Him to do (Day 5- John 5:18-20) and we are to fix our eyes on Him, the pioneer and perfecter of our faith. "Success is measured differently in the kingdom." What are your thoughts about how the Father sees success?

➤ Reflect and express below what God just showed you:

_____

_____

_____

_____

_____

_____

DAY 7:

➤ Take a moment to pray, then read the devotion again.

➤ Read Days 1-6 again in their entirety.

➤ Reflect on the past days and express below what God has revealed to you.

_____

_____

_____

_____

_____

Creative Expressions

I HAVE TRUST ISSUES

"Convincing work is the Spirit's work; he can do it effectually, and none but he."
-Matthew Henry

I have trust issues. I know that I must trust You with my kids, my job, my finances, my health, my marriage, yet I decide to step ahead of You and speak. So often I make a mess of it all.

I tend to create chaos.
You create peace.
Lord, help my unbelief.

Why do others seem to only see my nicely put-together life? I tell others to trust You, but I tend to find myself doing things to help You. I tend to create chaos. I must not believe that convincing is the Spirit's work. So often I decide to step ahead of You and speak.

Lord, help my unbelief.

I DO NOT have it all together. Some days I feel like one thread from becoming totally unraveled and other days the unraveled threads are miles apart, and I am walking around discombobulated trying to find a way to put the pieces back together.
I speak and create chaos.
You create peace.
Lord, help my unbelief.

My life is messy.

My life is unraveled.

My life is broken.

I want to say, "I hope you can relate," but that is a terrible thing to say. Yet I know some of you can relate.

I desperately want peace.

But somehow, I tend to create chaos.

Somehow, I tend to create the whirlwind.

Somehow…

Because I do not surrender.

Because I do not bow the knee.

Because I have trust issues.

I foolishly lift my head and speak more than bow my head in prayer.

I have trust issues.

Lord, help my unbelief.

DAILY TIME WITH GOD:

DAY 1:

➢ Take a moment to pray. Tell God that you know He is willing to speak, but you want to be willing to hear what He says to you today and every day. (James 1:5)

➢ Read the devotion again.

➢ Ponder the quote by Matthew Henry at the beginning of the devotion. Why are we so determined to either do the Holy Spirit's job or at the very least feel that we must help Him with the convincing work? What is our job? Are you doing that part well?

_____

_____

_____

_____

_____

DAY 2:

➤ Take a moment to pray. Isn't this the sweetest time to pray when you don't have a list but are just asking for Him to sit with you while you read?

➤ Read the devotion again.

➤ In what areas of your life do you wane in trusting God? List them, then scratch through each one and write "Surrender" beside it or on top of it. Take a moment as you do this and pray a prayer of surrender in each area. As you do this, know that you will have opportunities arise soon to show that you have surrendered that area to Him. We are not unaware of the enemy's schemes. He will want you to fail as soon as you begin to surrender to God, but remember God is on your side and has already provided the tools to win. Talk to Him about that as well right now, before the battle begins.

_____

_____

_____

_____

_____

DAY 3:

➤ Take a moment to pray using James 1:5 as your guide.

➤ Read the devotion again.

➤ When you do not trust God with a situation and you speak or act without His guidance, you have broken the designed order that He created; therefore, you are out of order, disorderly, creating chaos, etc. Do you see how you cannot have peace if you are not in line, in step, in the order He created? Talk to Him about that now. Express what He says to you as you ponder.

_____

_____

_____

_____

_____

DAY 4:

➤ Remember to take a moment to pray, then read the devotion again.

➤ "My life is messy. My life is unraveled. My life is broken." Do you feel like this is your life right now? Can you think of a time that a toddler got free reign in a room? It could be any room, but they typically make a mess of the order that was there before. They may not realize that they are creating chaos, but without guidance they will. If chaos, messiness, unraveling, or brokenness is a part of your life now, will you spend some time with God right now and ask Him to reveal where you have walked into a room (i.e., a situation) and not followed His guidance?

_____

_____

_____

_____

_____

DAY 5:

➤ Take a moment to pray and thank Him for His guidance.

➤ For a long time, I thought that the chaos was something that just kept happening to me. It was a victim mentality rather than an accountability mindset. Sometimes, we ever so quickly shift that blame right off our shoulders, don't we? We do not realize that we are speaking words that work against us. We do not realize that our actions have consequences and asking for forgiveness is appropriate, but unfortunately, we have already set the ungodly in motion. If we do not rise to take responsibility and stop it, it remains, ready to rise and create chaos again and again in our lives. Restoration is needed as well once we have disobeyed. Restoration is always at the heart of God. Talk to God about what you need to do to revoke access and restore the relationships both between you and Him, and between you and others.

_____

_____

_____

_____

_____

DAY 6

➢ Take a moment to pray. Tell God that you know He is willing to speak, but you want to be willing to hear what He says to you today and every day. (James 1:5)

➢ Read the devotion again.

➢ "I foolishly lift my head and speak more that bow my head in prayer. I have trust issues. Lord, help my unbelief." Many of us speak more than we pray. Take a moment to write out a declaration of trust in God that He can speak or move in a situation when you are being told to be silent. Make sure to include your devotion to prayer for we are not supposed to clam up but use our words in prayer. (Philippians 4:6)

_____

_____

_____

_____

_____

DAY 7:

➢ Take a moment to pray. His presence is invaluable.

➢ Read the devotion again.

➢ Read Days 1-6 again in their entirety.

➢ Reflect on the past days and express below what God has revealed to you.

_____

_____

_____

_____

_____

Creative Expressions

BREAKTHROUGH

"No weapon that is formed against you will succeed; And you will condemn every tongue that accuses you in judgment. This is the heritage of the servants of the LORD, And their vindication is from Me," declares the LORD.

Isaiah 54:17 (NASB)

W E E K   S E V E N
There Must Be A Power

I am learning a lot about myself lately.
I am afraid of failure, so I overwork.

I am afraid of rejection, so I blame my lack of commitment or contact with people on overworking.

I realize that I have fallen prey to the lies of the enemy, even though I know better. Obviously, knowing better does not always lead to success.

There must be a motivator greater than success, failure, or rejection because none of those work in the long run. If by chance, they do work, my body will probably not work under the enormous amount of stress that I have put on it when trying to achieve success under my own power.

There must be a power that moves me when I cannot motivate and move myself.

There must be a power that beckons me rather than drives me.

There must be a power greater than I, or I am lost.

There must be a power.

Power beyond me, but power from within that can motivate me.

A power that is immeasurable but condescends to meet my needs and knows my name.

A power that is indescribable but has a name.

There is such a power. His name is Holy Spirit.

I am learning more about Him.

He is powerful. He brings lasting change.

He beckons me. He motivates me.

I am learning about the Holy Spirit within me.

I am learning a lot about me.

Knowing Him changes everything.

There is hope for me. Christ in me, the hope of glory.

DAILY TIME WITH GOD:

DAY 1:

➢ Take a moment to pray. Tell God that you know He is willing to speak, but you want to be willing to hear what He says to you today and every day. (James 1:5)

➢ Read the devotion again.

"I am afraid of failure, so I overwork. I am afraid of rejection, so I blame my lack of commitment or contact with other people on overworking." Have you ever pondered why you do or why you do not do things in life? There is a reason. Ask God to show you one area that is not as you think it is. Ask Him to show you the true reason for your behavior. This revelation can help shift things in your life for the better once this pattern is broken.

_____

_____

_____

_____

_____

DAY 2:

➢ Take some time to pray before you read the devotion again.

➢ Why does *knowing better* not always lead to success? Are there any areas that God is speaking to you right now about in which you know better, but you are not motivated to change from just knowledge alone? Talk to Him about that one area right now. Reflect and express what God just revealed to you.

_____

_____

_____

_____

_____

DAY 3:

➢ Take a moment to pray, then read the devotion again.

➢ Do you realize the physical toll on your body from striving in your own power? We are fearfully and wonderfully made, yet there are limitations to the amount of stress and strain our fallen bodies can tolerate. Isaiah 9:6 says, "For to us a child is born, to us a son is given; and the government shall be upon his shoulder, and his name shall be called Wonderful Counselor, Mighty God, Everlasting Father, Prince of Peace." (ESV) Have you ever noticed the part in that verse that says that 'the government shall be upon his shoulder'? Neither your body, nor your shoulders were designed to take that kind of weight.[3] Governing the entire universe is an easy task for our Savior, but not for mortals like us. Talk to God about the weight on your shoulders. Reflect and express what God is saying to you.

_____

_____

_____

_____

DAY 4:

➢ Take a moment to pray. Using James 1:5 as your guide but talk to Him about anything else you want in this moment.

➢ Read the devotion again.

➢ I think we instinctively know that there is a power greater than ourselves and beyond ourselves, but it is amazing and humbling to know that that same power resides within ourselves! Reflect and express what God just revealed to you.

_____

_____

_____

_____

_____

DAY 5:

➢ Pray before you move onto the next step.

➢ Read the devotion again.

➢ The power within me and beyond me is not some impersonal force. He has a name. He knows your name. He wants to move within you to impact the world around you. Have you ever thought about that? Do you allow Him to do that? Reflect and express what God just revealed to you.

_____

_____

_____

_____

_____

DAY 6

➢ Take a moment to pray using James 1:5 as your guide.

➢ Read the devotion again.

➢ Knowing Him (the Holy Spirit) changes everything. He beckons us. He encourages us. He convicts us. He guides us. Continue listing things that the Holy Spirit does. If you cannot think of anything else, thank Him for the ones already listed.

_____

_____

_____

_____

_____

➢ Reflect and express what God just revealed to you.

_____

_____

_____

_____

_____

DAY 7:

➢ Today is the day to wrap it all up. We want His input to guide us and solidify what we learned this week so take that time to pray.
➢ Read the devotion again.
➢ Read Days 1-6 again in their entirety.
➢ Reflect on the past days and express below what God has revealed to you.

_____

_____

_____

_____

_____

Creative Expressions

FACTS VERSUS TRUTH

There is a vast difference between facts and truth.

Your peace lies in knowing the difference.

Facts can be listed and used to support your stance.

But the truths from God's word will trump all facts.

"Whining and complaining is the language of Satan", my pastor said.[4]

Your complaining may gain short-term results, but you have sided with the enemy for your victory. Therefore, you have no real victory.

We do not like to submit. We do not like to wait. We do not like to not be in control. Submitting the subpar situation to God and waiting on Him to move or speak goes against every fiber of our prideful selves, yet we continue to beseech the blessing of God amid our rebellion against His lordship. Heaven help us.

Satan will feed you many facts.

God will offer a higher truth.

Your peace lies in knowing the difference.

DAILY TIME WITH GOD:

DAY 1:

➤ Take a moment to pray. Tell God that you know He is willing to speak, but you want to be willing to hear what He says to you today and every day. (James 1:5)

➤ Read the devotion again.

➤ Do you understand the difference between facts and truth as talked about in the devotion? Do you find yourself trusting more in the facts of a situation rather than searching for God's truth? Reflect and express what God just revealed to you.

_____

_____

_____

_____

_____

DAY 2:

➤ Take a moment to pray before you read the devotion again.

➤ The word 'Satan' is a Hebrew word for "adversary." Miriam-Webster dictionary offers synonyms for the word 'adversary' as a noun: antagonist, enemy, foe, hostile, opponent; synonyms when used as an adjective: adversarial, antagonistic, hostile, inhospitable, negative, unfriendly, unsympathetic. After thinking about the synonyms for Satan, why would it be appropriate for my pastor to say, "Whining and complaining is the language of Satan?" Have you ever thought about whining and complaining in that way?

➤ Reflect and express what God just revealed to you.

_____

_____

_____

_____

_____

Day 3:

➢ Take a moment to pray. Tell God that you know He is willing to speak, but you want to be willing to hear what He says to you today and every day. (James 1:5)

➢ Read the devotion again.

➢ "Your complaining may gain short-term results, but you have sided with the enemy for your victory. Therefore, you have no real victory."

➢ Sit and ponder the previous quote. The facts make it look like you have a victory, but does God offer a better way? Think about the last time you felt like you achieved a victory, but you used Satan's tools. Confess that sin to God and ask Him to reveal the Godly way you could have responded instead. Write what He shows you.

_____

_____

_____

_____

Day 4:

➢ Take a moment to pray. Today, thank Him specifically that He is willing to speak. (James 1:5)

➢ Read the devotion again.

➢ The Bible says that the fruit of the Spirit is love, joy, peace, patience, kindness, goodness, faithfulness, gentleness and self-control. Short-term victories handled Satan's way would happen less often if we focused on growing the fruit of the Spirit in our lives.

➢ I hear a lot of people say they need to be more patient. Yes, we should be more patient with God, more patient with others, and more patient with ourselves. Yet, if we loved others as God loves them, it would be much easier to be kind, gentle, patient and self-controlled. The *fruit* are not meant to be used in isolation.

➢ Write out how you could incorporate a few of the fruit of the Spirit into the situation you had previously referenced where you did not handle it God's way. For example, "I will focus more on my love for the other person, which would compel me to respond with kindness and patience instead of judgment and criticism."

_____

_____

_____

_____

_____

Day 5:

➢ Take a moment to pray and read the devotion again.

➢ "…we continue to beseech the blessing of God amid our rebellion against His lordship." The word 'Lord' seems archaic to us. In modern day terms, it would be almost the equivalent to a boss or a person of high rank or position, such as a king or queen. If a person of high rank or position walked into the room, would you remain seated and continue eating or talking or would you stand and silently acknowledge their position or title? In the physical world, we would not continue to beseech a king's blessing while we were actively rebelling against the honor and deference due his title. God is the King of kings and Lord of lords. Are you "beseeching His blessing amid your rebellion against His lordship?"

➢ Reflect and express what God just revealed to you.

_____

_____

_____

_____

_____

Day 6

➢ Remember that His presence makes the difference between reading for information and growing in wisdom from what you read or experience. Take the time to pray and ask Him to be with you, then read the devotion again.

➢ Consider these sentences from the devotion:
"Facts can be listed and used to support your stance.
But the truths from God's word will trump all facts.
Satan will feed you many facts.
God will offer a higher truth.
Your peace lies in knowing the difference."

➢ Spend time with the Lord right now. Talk to Him about giving you wisdom and discernment to know how to balance facts and truth, and the ability to respond and speak the way He desires.

_____

_____

_____

_____

_____

➢ Reflect and express what God just revealed to you.

_____

_____

_____

_____

_____

DAY 7:

➢ Take a moment to pray using James 1:5 as your guide, then read the devotion again.
➢ Read Days 1-6 again in their entirety.
➢ Reflect on the past days and express below what God has revealed to you.

_____

_____

_____

_____

_____

Creative Expressions

It's Not Working

It's not working.

This thing in my life is not working.

I have been emotional all week because I cannot see any other way to make it work.

If I did not love it so much, it I would not hurt so much. I must love it very much for it hurts so badly.

Yet, it is not working.

As I lie here, tearful, and emotional over what I am about to lose, I get a thought.

What if God is not wanting me to give up what I love but wants me to give up what is not working?

What if I have not given Him lordship over it and whatever usurps His place is an idol?

What if He is showing me that idols are not Him, and therefore, they will never work?

What if He is giving me the opportunity to skim the dross to possess the pure silver?

What if God wants to be God and show Himself strong for those who call upon His name?

What if God wants to lift the needy out of the dung hill and set their feet on solid ground?

What if I just let all of my idols fall, let God be God and go to sleep in peace?

Sleep in peace tonight, my friend. And if something is not working, trust the One who loves you the most and surrender it to Him.

It is not working for a reason.

DAILY TIME WITH GOD

DAY 1:

➢ Take a moment to pray. Tell God that you know He is willing to speak, but you want to be willing to hear what He says to you today and every day. (James 1:5)
➢ Read the devotion again.
➢ Is there something(s) in your life that you feel is not working? List them below. Use a code if you do not want to write it all out. God will know what you are talking about.

_____

_____

_____

_____

_____

DAY 2:

➢ Is the habit of praying before you read getting easier? Remember, when you practice something over and over again, it becomes easier to keep that skill in your life.
➢ Read the devotion again.
➢ Have you lamented over something more than you have prayed over it? You can be sorrowful over something, but does that sorrow only lead you to much more sorrow? Make a list of responses that are better than sorrow. Here are a few examples to get you thinking: prayer, talking to a Godly friend, journaling.

_____

_____

_____

_____

_____

➤ Reflect and express what God just revealed to you.

_____

_____

_____

_____

DAY 3:

➤ Take a moment to pray and read the devotion again.
➤ Have you ever realized that God may not be wanting you to give up something as much as He wants you to give it to Him? Talk to Him about that now.
➤ Pray for strength and discernment to recognize when you are not giving something to Him.
➤ Reflect and express what God is saying to you.

_____

_____

_____

_____

DAY 4:

➤ Take a moment to pray, then read the devotion again. Hopefully, praying before you read has become more rooted in your life as we have moved through this book.
➤ An idol is anything that takes the place of God. If you have an area of your life that you have not given to Him, then that area is not under His lordship. Since idols are not God, they cannot give us what we need. List any area of your life that you have not given Him complete control of, then beside each one, prayerfully write the words, "Surrendered to You

today" and date it. Make sure you take time to confess your lordship errors, but remember, God always has a view toward reconciliation. Let Him speak life into you and into that area of your life. Let Him be Lord today over every aspect of your life. God is not condemning you, therefore, speak life to yourself as well.

_____

_____

_____

_____

_____

DAY 5:

➤ Take a moment to pray. Tell God that you know He is willing to speak, but you want to be willing to hear what He says to you today and every day. (James 1:5)

➤ Read the devotion again.

➤ "What if He is giving me the opportunity to skim the dross to possess the pure silver?" Dross is the impurities in silver. When silver is heated, the dross comes to the top and a silversmith can then skim the dross off the top, thereby removing the impurities.

➤ Sometimes when we face difficulties, we question if we heard God and are in the right place. Maybe God has brought us to a place and even though it is a gift from Him, that area of our life can become contaminated. Therefore, He needs to purify it for it to remain holy and acceptable to Him. Other times, He is moving us to a new chapter, a new season, or a new level. There is a difference between refining and moving. Spend time with your heavenly Father and ask if He is removing things from your life or is He only removing the impurities ("skimming the dross") from that area? If He is indeed only refining or "skimming the dross" from an area, write out your response to this process. As you ponder and wait on the Lord, He will reveal more and more to you as you are ready to receive it.

_____

_____

_____

_____

_____

DAY 6

➢ Take a moment to pray. Listen for what He says. When you are ready, read the devotion again.

➢ It is sometimes easy to say that you surrender it all to Him, but the proof is in your actions and in your ability to sleep in peace tonight. After all the work this week on letting go and surrendering it to God, your sleep should be peaceful tonight. Thank Him for His sovereign care over you and your life. Thank Him for peaceful sleep.

_____

_____

_____

_____

_____

DAY 7:

➢ Take a moment to pray. Thank Him for being willing to speak, then read the devotion again.

➢ Read Days 1-6 again in their entirety.

➢ Reflect on the past days and express below what God has revealed to you.

_____

_____

_____

_____

_____

Creative Expressions

THE PONDERING FOCUS

....

You may be surprised to know that we were created to ponder. As I stated earlier in this book, pondering at its core is deliberately pausing to notice, however, all the pondering in the world is worthless without God. God makes all things good. God is goodness embodied therefore; He is the ultimate goal of our pondering.

"The LORD made the earth by his power, and he preserves it by his wisdom. With his own understanding he stretched out the heavens." Jeremiah 51:15 (NLT)

"For by him all things were created, in heaven and on earth, visible and invisible, whether thrones or dominions or rulers or authorities—all things were created through him and for him. And he is before all things, and in him all things hold together." Colossians 1: 16-17 (ESV)

*"For this reason [grasping the greatness of this plan by which Jews and Gentiles are joined together in Christ] I bow my knees [in reverence] before the Father [of our Lord Jesus Christ], from whom every family in heaven and on earth derives its name [God--the first and ultimate Father]. May He grant you out of the riches of His glory, to be strengthened and spiritually energized with power through His Spirit in your inner self, [indwelling your innermost being and personality], so that Christ may dwell in your hearts through your faith. And may you, having been [deeply] rooted and [securely] grounded in love, be fully capable of comprehending with all the saints (God's people) the width and length and height and depth of His love [fully experiencing that amazing, endless love]; and [that you may come] to know [practically, through personal experience] the love of Christ **which far surpasses [mere] knowledge** [without experience], that you may be filled up [throughout your being] to all the fullness of God [so that you may have the richest experience of God's presence in your lives, completely filled and flooded with God Himself]..."* Ephesians 3:14-19 (AMP) (emphasis mine)

To know the love of Christ in a way that "far surpasses [mere] knowledge" sounds supernatural, but I believe that we can also find it in the natural through stillness and presence. Maybe that is why Psalms 46:10 says,

> *"Be still and know (recognize, understand) that I am God. I will be exalted among the nations! I will be exalted in the earth." (AMP)*

We ponder the goodness of God.

That is what we are called to do.

That is what we are created to do.

Take a moment to ponder what you just read. Close your eyes and breathe. Ponder who you were created to be for a moment. Use this space to express what you feel about your Creator right now. If you do not feel creative, then simply but creatively write, "Thank You."

IDENTITY

See what great love the Father has lavished on us, that we should be called children of God! And that is what we are!

1 John 3:1 (NIV)

IDENTITY CHANGES EVERYTHING

God began to speak to me about identity a couple of years ago. I realized very quickly that identity changes everything. He showed me that I am an *ambassador* from His kingdom in this world. I do not think of myself as an ambassador, but that is who I am.

> *"Therefore, we are ambassadors for Christ, as though God were making an appeal through us; we beg you on behalf of Christ, be reconciled to God." 2 Corinthians 5:20 (NASB)*

Do you know who you are?

Identity changes everything.

I began to think more and more about my identity as a child of God. I do not always act like a child of God, but actions and identity are different. They should not be different, but they can be.

When you know who you are, you realize that failures do not define you.

When you know who God is, you realize that God wants to refine you through your failures and more importantly, He still loves you through your failures.

The enemy knows the importance of identity, and that is why he attacks it relentlessly. The enemy is quick to point out when we do not look like, act like nor sound like a child of God, therefore, it is imperative to know your identity. I have not always acted like my parents, nor have I always acted like they wanted me to act, but it did not change my identity. Each time I did not act like them, I was still their child. No matter the external circumstances, I will remain their child.

Identity is a powerful weapon. Saturate yourself with God's word so that when the enemy speaks, you can discern conviction from condemnation. Condemnation is designed to be a destructive attack on your identity. Conviction is designed to spur you to return to your identity as a child of God.

> *"See what great love the Father has lavished on us, that we should be called children of God! And that is what we are!" 1 John 3:1a (NIV)*

This is how you should think of yourself:

> I know who I am.
> I am a spokesperson for God.
> I am an ambassador from the Kingdom of light, and I represent Him well.
> I allow his power to flow through me and His power always brings about change.
> I am an avid reader of His word so that I am always aware of my authority and jurisdiction.
> I know who I am.
>
> Do you know who you are?
> Identity changes everything.

DAILY TIME WITH GOD

DAY 1:

➢ Take a moment to pray. Tell God that you know He is willing to speak, but you want to be willing to hear what He says to you today and every day. (James 1:5)
➢ Read the devotion again.
➢ Before you read this devotion, had you ever thought of yourself as an ambassador for Christ? What do you think about that now? How well do you represent His kingdom? If you do

not feel that you have represented Him well, write out a declaration stating that you are aware and are equipped to do your job well as of today. He does not want the lingering thoughts of yourself to be of failure, my friend. Be kind to yourself on this journey.

_____

_____

_____

_____

_____

DAY 2:

➢ Make sure you pray, even if it is just a quick request of the Father to be with you. He knows what you are going through.

➢ Read the devotion again.

➢ Why does identity change everything? For example, would you act, talk and even walk differently if you were an owner of a business or only an employee there? Take time to reflect on your identity in Christ. You may even want to search for a list on "I am" statements on who you are in Christ. The book of Colossians has many as well. Write out a few that resonate with you below.

_____

_____

_____

_____

_____

DAY 3:

➤ Pray, then read the devotion again.

➤ Do you feel that your failures define you? Do you feel that what God says about you defines you and your failures are meant to refine you? Take a moment to ponder your thoughts about yourself. Pray and ask God to allow you to see yourself how He sees you. Then write out a declaration to never allow the enemy to define you.

_____

_____

_____

_____

_____

DAY 4:

➤ Take a moment to pray. Tell God that you know He is willing to speak, but you want to be willing to hear what He says to you today and every day. (James 1:5)

➤ Read the devotion again.

➤ "The enemy knows how important identity is." Do you realize that the enemy knows exactly what would happen if you truly knew your identity and acted in line with that knowledge? Do you know who you are? "Identity changes everything."

➤ Write out a few statements of who you are. If you absolutely feel that you cannot come up with some on your own, then rewrite the ones that are in this devotion.

_____

_____

_____

_____

_____

DAY 5:

➢ Invite your heavenly Father to your pondering time today, then read the devotion again.

➢ "Saturate yourself with God's word so that when the enemy speaks, you can discern conviction from condemnation. Condemnation is designed to be a destructive attack on your identity. Conviction is designed to spur you to return to your identity as a child of God." Do you realize how important God's word is to your identity? Do you truly realize that? If you do, then you understand why the enemy works relentlessly to keep you from God's word.

➢ Reflect and express what God just revealed to you.

_____

_____

_____

_____

_____

DAY 6

➢ Take a moment to pray. Thank Him for His Word and His guidance.

➢ Read the devotion again.

➢ "Condemnation is designed to be a destructive attack on your identity. Conviction is designed to spur you to return to your identity as a child of God." Do you realize that the same situation can bring condemnation or conviction? Which one depends on whose voice you are listening to. Condemnation tends to be a global attack on you as a person. For example, you will hear yourself say things like, "I am horrible. I can't believe I would ever behave that way." Conviction is allowing God to shine His light on one specific area that He knows you can conquer, for He would not highlight it just to make you feel bad. Recognize the enemy's tactics.

➢ Reflect and express what God just revealed to you.

_____

_____

_____

_____

_____

Day 7:

➢ Take a moment to pray using James 1:5 as your guide.

➢ Read the devotion again.

➢ Read Days 1-6 again in their entirety.

➢ Reflect on the past days and express below what God has revealed to you.

_____

_____

_____

_____

_____

Creative Expressions

WHERE ARE YOU LOOKING?

"If you look at the world, you'll be distressed. If you look within, you'll be depressed. But if you look at Christ, you'll be at rest." Corrie ten Boom

Today I needed to hear her words.

Today I need to rest in Him.

Today I will be still.

Amidst the destruction, devastation, and the never-ending requests for help, I need to rest in Him.

I cannot continue to serve out of a dry cistern. I need to be filled with Him.

Almost 20 years ago, during bed rest while pregnant for my daughter, God brought me to Psalm 84:6:

> *"As they go through the Valley of Baca they make it a place of springs; the early rain also covers it with pools." (ESV)*

"The vale of Baca was some waterless and barren valley through which pilgrims passed on their way to Jerusalem; but faith turns it into a place of springs, finding refreshment under the most untoward circumstances, while God refreshes them with showers of blessing from above, as the autumnal rains clothe the dry plains with grass and flowers"[5]

"...by the presence of the Saviour, by the influence of the Holy Spirit, the Comforter, such times become seasons of purest joy - times remembered ever afterward with most fervent gratitude, as among the happiest periods of life"[6]

Let my face be towards You in all circumstances so I may feel Your presence.

Let my faith be in You when I am dry and weary so I may stand and serve in Your strength.

Let my fears be subdued by Your voice so I may walk in peace and pass that peace on to those I meet.

Let my faults be brought before You for forgiveness and restoration so that I may forgive others.

Let my life be a reflection of You to a dry and thirsty world.

Refreshing rain. Renewing Presence. Restoring grace.

Fill me. Refresh me. Renew me.

DAILY TIME WITH GOD

DAY 1:

➢ Take a moment to pray. Tell God that you know He is willing to speak, but you want to be willing to hear what He says to you today and every day. (James 1:5)
➢ Read the devotion again.
➢ Ponder the quote from Corrie Ten Boom. Do you know her story? A brief part of her story consists of being imprisoned during the Holocaust. Her father and sister died in the concentration camps. She has written books on her experience, not only in the Holocaust and the concentration camps, but her experience with God as well. Ponder her quote again with this new knowledge.

_____

_____

_____

_____

_____

DAY 2:

➤ Take a moment to pray. Remind Him of your willingness to sit and listen for His voice then read the devotion again.

➤ "Amidst the destruction, devastation, and the never-ending requests for help, I need to rest in Him. I cannot continue to serve out of a dry cistern. I need to be filled, with Him." I wrote this devotion when our area had been hit by two hurricanes within weeks of each other. I, along with my family and my surrounding area, felt depleted. The people who were impacted were helping others who were impacted because we all needed help in the midst of needing help. It was such an odd season. Living amid destruction and devastation made it difficult to recharge. Are you in a season where there is destruction, devastation, and never-ending requests for help? Do you find time to rest in Him, because "you cannot continue to serve out of a dry cistern?" Pause and ponder these things. If you feel led by God to write or express what He shows below.

_____

_____

_____

_____

_____

DAY 3:

➤ Take a moment to pray, then read the devotion again.

➤ "The vale of Baca was some waterless and barren valley through which pilgrims passed on their way to Jerusalem; but faith turns it into a place of springs, finding refreshment under the most untoward circumstances, while God refreshes them with showers of blessing from above, as the autumnal rains clothe the dry plains with grass and flowers." What do you think about this commentary on Psalm 84:6?

➤ What part did God highlight to you?

_____

_____

_____

_____

_____

➤ Reflect and express what God is saying to you.

_____

_____

_____

_____

_____

DAY 4:

➤ Take as much time as you need today when praying. We are in no hurry to get to our pondering.

➤ Read the devotion again.

➤ "...by the presence of the Saviour, by the influence of the Holy Spirit, the Comforter, such times become seasons of purest joy - times remembered ever afterward with most fervent gratitude, as among the happiest periods of life." What do you think about this commentary on Psalm 84:6?

➤ What part did God highlight to you?

_____

_____

_____

_____

_____

➤ Reflect and express what God is saying to you.

_____
_____
_____
_____
_____

DAY 5:

➤ Take a moment to pray. Tell God that you know He is willing to speak, but you want to be willing to hear what He says to you today and every day. (James 1:5)
➤ Read the devotion again.
➤ Read each one of the following statements out loud, pausing to pray after each one. Then take the time to write each one as a declaration to God.
  • Let my face be towards You in all circumstances so I may feel Your presence.
  • Let my faith be in You when I am dry and weary so I may stand and serve in Your strength.
  • Let my fears be subdued by Your voice so I may walk in peace and pass it on to those I meet.
  • Let my faults be brought before You for forgiveness and restoration so that I may forgive others.
  • Let my life be a reflection of You to a dry and thirsty world.

_____
_____
_____
_____
_____

➤ Reflect and express anything else that God may have revealed to you.

_____
_____

_____

_____

_____

DAY 6

➢ Take a moment to pray, then read the devotion again.

➢ Take time to thank Him for these: "Refreshing rain. Renewing presence. Restoring grace."

➢ Take time to ask for these: "Fill me. Refresh me. Renew me."

➢ Reflect and express what God just revealed to you.

_____

_____

_____

_____

_____

DAY 7:

➢ Take a moment to pray using James 1:5 as your guide.

➢ Read the devotion again.

➢ Read Days 1-6 again in their entirety.

➢ Reflect on the past days and express below what God has revealed to you.

_____

_____

_____

_____

Creative Expressions

WHERE ARE YOU SEATED TODAY?

Do not let your circumstances be bigger than Your God for that is how you lose your peace and your joy.

I once heard a famous pastor say something like this one day, 'Storms were not designed to sink you. They are designed to show you the power that God has placed within you.'

> *"The men were amazed and asked, "What kind of man is this? Even the winds and the waves obey him!" Matthew 8:27 (NIV)*

> *"And God raised us up with Christ and seated us with him in the heavenly realms in Christ Jesus," Eph. 2:6 (NIV)*

Being seated in the heavenlies has very clear advantages.

That is where you are.

That is where storms are not.

In the heavenlies are peace and joy.

In His presence there is protection, peace, and provision.

Where are you seated today?

DAILY TIME WITH GOD

DAY 1:

➤ Take a moment to pray. Tell God that you know He is willing to speak, but you want to be willing to hear what He says to you today and every day. (James 1:5)

➤ Read the devotion again.

➤ How big are your circumstances compared to God? How big is God compared to your circumstances?

_____

_____

_____

_____

_____

➤ Look at what you wrote or expressed creatively and evaluate whether you believe this based on your actions and your speech. Express your answer below or in the margins.

_____

_____

_____

_____

_____

DAY 2:

➤ Take a moment to pray using James 1:5 as your guide, then read the devotion again.

➤ Read Romans 8:38-39. Have you lost peace and joy by letting your circumstances be bigger than your God?

➤ Reflect and express what God has shown you:

_____

_____

_____

_____

_____

DAY 3:

➤ Pray with thankfulness in your heart today, then read the devotion again.

➤ When did the disciples turn to Him in Matthew 8:23-27? When a storm comes into your life, is your first reaction to think that you are sinking, or do you immediately turn to Him?

_____

_____

_____

_____

_____

➤ Reflect and express what God has shown you:

_____

_____

_____

_____

_____

DAY 4:

➤ Take a moment to pray. Tell God that you know He is willing to speak, but you want to be willing to hear what He says to you today and every day. (James 1:5)

➤ Read the devotion again.

➤ "For he raised us from the dead along with Christ and seated us with him in the heavenly realms because we are united with Christ Jesus." Eph. 2:6 (NLT)

➤ What does it mean to be seated in heavenly places? Stop for a moment and visualize yourself seated in heavenly places. If you feel led, respond below with what God shows you.

_____

_____

_____

_____

_____

DAY 5:

➢ Are you able to take a few moments to pray each day before you get into the readings? Take that time now then read the devotion again.

➢ Revelation 21:4 reads, "He will wipe away every tear from their eyes, and there will no longer be any death; there will no longer be any mourning or crying or pain." (NASB) Why are there no storms in heaven, physically or spiritually?

_____

_____

_____

_____

_____

➢ Reflect and express what God has shown you:

_____

_____

_____

_____

_____

DAY 6

➢ Take a moment to pray thanking Him for being who He is.
➢ Read the devotion again.

➢ In His presence there is protection, peace and provision.
- Protection: Isaiah 41:10 says, "Do not fear, for I am with you; Do not anxiously look about you, for I am your God. I will strengthen you, surely I will help you, Surely I will uphold you with My righteous right hand." (NASB)
- Peace: 2 Thessalonians 3:16 reads, "Now may the Lord of peace Himself continually grant you peace in every circumstance. The Lord be with you all!" (NASB)
- Provision: Philippians 4:19 says, "And my God will supply all your needs according to His riches in glory in Christ Jesus." (NASB)

➢ Reflect and express what God has shown you:

_____

_____

_____

_____

DAY 7:

➢ Take a moment to pray. Tell God that you know He is willing to speak, but you want to be willing to hear what He says to you today and every day. (James 1:5)

➢ Read the devotion again.

➢ Read Days 1-6 again in their entirety.

➢ Reflect on the past days and express below what God has revealed to you.

_____

_____

_____

_____

_____

Creative Expressions

HOPE

May the God of hope fill you with all joy and peace as you trust in him, so that you may overflow with hope by the power of the Holy Spirit.

Romans 15:13 (NIV)

I Choose To Believe

Hope is what I choose to hang my hat on. The voice of the enemy tells me that my situations are hopeless. Without the frame of reference of how big God is, situations can easily feel hopeless. Instead of talking about how big your problems are, talk about the magnitude of your God.

Listen to how Isaiah describes God,

> *Who has measured the waters in the hollow of His hand, And marked off the heavens with a span [of the hand], And calculated the dust of the earth with a measure, And weighed the mountains in a balance And the hills in a pair of scales? Isaiah 40:12 (AMP)*

It says that God can measure the heavens with the span of His hand. The word hand is singular. One hand. One hand can measure the heavens. I have a difficult time imagining man traveling to the moon, much less to the outside of the galaxies where God is. Yes, I know that God is not located in one place, but just think through the wording of this verse. It specifically designates that one of His hands is measuring the inconceivable. My finite mortal mind struggles with these concepts. Keeping in step with this verse, I cannot grasp the *size* of my God or where He is standing if the galaxies are in His hands, yet I only need to fill my mind with what He has revealed to me. I read His words, I listen to His voice, I watch His plans unfold, and I can sit so close to the unimaginably large God to feel His goodness toward those He loves, and that includes me!

He loves me. Wayward, fickle me, who messes up again and again. On those awful days that I live below my victory, I can choose to hang my hat on His words; words that are filled with love and hope; words for me. I can choose to let His words become the thoughts that roll around in my head. I can fill my mind to the brim with words that speak of the goodness of God so that despair and depression have no place to lay their head.

The enemy preys on our ignorance. We need to study God and His ways, His love and His grace, His kindness and goodness, His blessings and presence. Determine that His voice is worth shutting out all the other voices.

Choose.

I choose to believe what God says.

I choose to listen to His voice.

I choose Him.

And He has chosen me.

I am my beloved's, and He is mine.

I do not think I will ever understand why He has chosen to connect Himself to me.

But I choose to believe He has, and He has promised good to me.

I choose to believe.

It is quite simple.

I choose You, dear Lord.

I choose You.

DAILY TIME WITH GOD:

DAY 1:

➢ Take a moment to pray. Tell God that you know He is willing to speak, but you want to be willing to hear what He says to you today and every day. (James 1:5)

➢ Read the devotion again.

➢ Jesus said, "My sheep hear my voice, and I know them, and they follow me" John 10:27 (ESV) Can you discern the enemy's voice from His voice? What are some tell-tale signs that it is the enemy's voice (fear, hopelessness, etc....)?

_____

_____

_____

_____

_____

➤ What does God's voice sound like to you? It may not sound like an audible voice, but Jesus said that His sheep know His voice, so it can be heard. How do you hear Him?

_____

_____

_____

_____

_____

➤ Reflect and express what God has shown you:

_____

_____

_____

_____

_____

DAY 2:

➤ Take a moment to pray. Thank Him that you were created to hear His voice and you are listening.

➤ Read the devotion again.

➤ We need to study God's word so that we can train our ears to hear His voice. Here are some examples of what He says to us,

"The Lord, the Lord God, merciful and gracious, longsuffering, and abounding in goodness and truth." Exodus 34:6 (NKJV)

"Oh, give thanks to the LORD, for *He is* good! For His mercy *endures* forever." 1 Chronicles 16:34 (NKJV)

"Surely goodness and mercy shall follow me all the days of my life, and I shall dwell in the house of the LORD forever." Psalm 23:6 (ESV)

➢ Hearing these few scriptures begins to retrain our ears and our mind to the truth regarding what He thinks about you. Knowing this, is His voice worth shutting out all other voices? Reflect and express what God has shown you:

_____

_____

_____

_____

_____

Day 3:

➢ Take a moment to pray using James 1:5 as your guide.
➢ Read the devotion again.
➢ Look back at the scripture reference from the devotion, then read this scripture: "When I look at your heavens, the work of your fingers, the moon and the stars, which you have set in place, what is man that you are mindful of him, and the son of man that you care for him?" Psalm 8:3-4 (ESV). Today, I want you to ponder the *size* of God and the size of His love for you.
➢ Reflect and express what God has shown you:

_____

_____

_____

_____

_____

DAY 4:

➤ Take a moment to pray. Thank Him for creating the heavens, the moon and the stars. Thank Him for creating you.

➤ Read the devotion again.

➤ Ponder this sentence from the devotion: "I will fill my thoughts with the goodness of God so that despair and depression have no place to lay their head." Renewing your mind with what He says and keeping your mind stayed on Him is the way you win the battle for your thoughts.

Isaiah 26:3 reads, "You keep him in perfect peace whose mind is stayed on you, because he trusts in you." (ESV)

Romans 12:2 reads, "Don't copy the behavior and customs of this world, but let God transform you into a new person by changing the way you think. Then you will learn to know God's will for you, which is good and pleasing and perfect." (NLT)

➤ Reflect and express what God has shown you:

_____

_____

_____

_____

_____

DAY 5:

➤ Take a moment to pray. Tell God that you know He is willing to speak, but you want to be willing to hear what He says to you today and every day. (James 1:5)

➤ Read the devotion again.

➤ Isaiah 40:12 reads, "Who has measured the waters in the hollow of His hand, And marked off the heavens with a span [of the hand], And calculated the dust of the earth with a measure, And weighed the mountains in a balance And the hills in a pair of scales?" (ESV)

➤ Did you note the references to God's hand in the verses? How *big* does it make Him seem? (Again, I know that God cannot be measured, but consider what He is doing in this verse: measuring the heavens with the span of His hand). Now, compare how *big* God is to the size of your problems. This exercise is not to force you think that your problems are inconsequential to a vast and incomprehensible God. On the contrary, He specifically tells us that He is aware and concerned with the swallow and the blade of grass. Therefore, I am certain He is mindful of us and our situations, I just wanted to get you rightly aligned with your Creator.

➢ Reflect and express what God has shown you:

_____

_____

_____

_____

DAY 6

➢ Pause for a moment before getting into the reading today and pray. It is worth your time.
➢ Read the devotion again.
➢ *Choose* is a powerful word. What does it mean to you that He has chosen you and you have chosen Him?
➢ Choosing God is not just a one-time choice. Choosing Him means a lifetime commitment to a relationship with Him. Why is commitment important to your relationship with Him? Does your current level of commitment need to increase? If so, how can you tangibly do that? Reflect and express what God has shown you:

_____

_____

_____

_____

DAY 7:

➢ Take a moment to pray. Tell God that you know He is willing to speak, but you want to be willing to hear what He says to you today and every day. (James 1:5)
➢ Read the devotion again.

➤ Read Days 1-6 again in their entirety.

➤ Reflect on the past days and express below what God has revealed to you.

_____

_____

_____

_____

_____

Creative Expressions

Better Days Are Coming

"Staying positive doesn't mean you have to be happy all the time. It means that even on hard days you know that there are better ones coming."[8]

Hard days.

The prophet Jeremiah was experiencing hard days. The children of Israel were experiencing the same. It was not a happy time.

Judgment had been forecasted to the people of God if repentance did not occur. The Israelites had remained disobedient, so the long-suffering of God had come to an end and the unthinkable had happened; the people of God had been captured and brought to live in another land. On that day, I would suppose that they were bewildered and filled with despair. When your whole world comes crashing down around you, hanging your head in despair would be the natural response. It is not a person's first reaction to look for the silver lining when the dark cloud has recently descended. It is not a person's first reaction to look up and be hopeful when devastation of that magnitude occurs. When calamity comes, survival is your first thought.

Dark clouds filled their skies and the horizon looked dismal and long; better days must have seemed so far away. But God knows what is behind those clouds. God knows our future and He knows that clouds move. God knows what all your tomorrows hold. Since God is kind and compassionate, He will never leave us without hope. He didn't leave His people without hope either.

"For I know the thoughts that I think toward you, says the Lord, thoughts of peace and not of evil, to give you a future and a hope. Then you will call upon Me and go and pray to Me, and I will listen to you. And you will seek Me and find Me, when you search for Me with all your heart." Jeremiah 29:11-13 (NKJV)

Let's go back for moment, before calamity, before captivity. Can you imagine the day the Israelites heard the approaching army; the army that God had told them was going to come in response to their disobedience? I can imagine their emotional response was of fear and dread. But have you ever thought about their physical response? Do you realize your physical response when bad news comes in? In working with individuals who have experienced severe trauma, I work with the body as well as the mind for they go into the trauma together, therefore, both the body and mind need to come out of the trauma together.

When hearing bad news, a sharp inhale is a natural response. It is the same response a baby has as the doctor tilts their body backwards right after coming out of the womb. The baby inhales sharply in response to the sudden tilt backwards, then their arms and legs move outward and away from the body. It is called the Moro reflex. The remnants of it remain throughout our life and is unconsciously reactivated in sudden stress.

Sudden stress. I can only imagine the sharp inhale as the children of God heard the approaching army. The sound of marching feet, horses and chariot wheels would have been enough to reactivate the Moro reflex for me.

We live in a fallen world and the unexplainable and the seemingly unbearable happens. Has that time come upon you? A time of unexpected bad news, unexplainable loss, or pain so severe that takes your breath away? I can imagine that sharp inhale because I have experienced it as well. On days when despair seems so heavy and thick that I cannot move forward, I need to stop, breathe, and refocus on God.

On the other side of hanging your head is looking up.

On the other side of inhaling is exhaling.

On the other side of fear is a God who never left.

Inhale. Exhale.

It's a simple task.

Inhale. Exhale.

Inhale. Exhale.

Sometimes it's all we can do, but we must never lose sight of God's ultimate plans.

"For I know the thoughts that I think toward you, says the Lord, thoughts of peace and not of evil, to give you a future and a hope. Then you will call upon Me and go and pray to Me, and I will listen to you. And you will seek Me and find Me, when you search for Me with all your heart." Jeremiah 29:11-13 (NKJV)

Cry. Grieve. Moan. Sigh.

Inhale. Exhale.

Remember, better days are coming. Praise Him. Raise your hands. Shout a hallelujah. For God, in His infinite mercy, does not leave us without hope, ever. God knows every detail of our future and He has a plan for every one of us.

On the days when the enemy wants me to hang my head in despair, I can choose to lift my head and focus on the hope that He has put within me through the victorious work of Jesus. Jesus has overcome; better days are coming.

We know the end of the story; better days are coming. It does not matter what today holds nor what news comes my way, God's word tells me to lift my head, better days are coming. I may not be able to choose the details of the day, but I can choose to focus on the One who has a glorious future marked out for me despite the details of the day. Better days are coming.

God has given us breath to live, to praise, to laugh, to cry, to moan in anguish, but the focus in all our breathing must remain constant and steady on the One who gave us breath.

Pick your head up.

Breathe.

Better days are coming.

DAILY TIME WITH GOD

DAY 1:

➤ Take a moment to pray. Tell God that you know He is willing to speak, but you want to be willing to hear what He says to you today and every day. (James 1:5)

➤ Read the devotion again.

➤ Do you love God's word? Do you love to pick it up and read it? If not, where do you find your joy and hope?

_____

_____

_____

_____

_____

➤ Write out a prayer of confession or declaration based on your love for God's word.

_____

_____

_____

_____

DAY 2:

➤ Take a moment to pray. Thank Him for His Word. Thank Him that you have time to study it and learn more about Him.

➤ Read the devotion again.

➤ Write out Jeremiah 29:11-13 below. We pondered these verses last week in response to hope. How does this verse relate to "better days are coming?"

_____

_____

_____

_____

_____

➤ Reflect and express what God just revealed to you.

_____

_____

_____

_____

_____

DAY 3:

➤ Take a moment to pray using James 1:5 as your guide.
➤ Read the devotion again.
➤ Why is God so intent on blessing our future despite our failures, flaws and fickle devotion to Him? Lamentations 3:22 reads, "Because of the LORD's great love we are not consumed, for his compassions never fail." (NIV)
➤ Reflect and express what God just revealed to you.

_____

_____

_____

_____

_____

DAY 4:

➤ Take a moment to pray. Thank Him for His faithfulness to you.
➤ Read the devotion again.
➤ Philippians 3:13-14 reads, "Brothers and sisters, I do not consider myself to have attained this. Instead, I am single-minded: Forgetting the things that are behind and reaching

out for the things that are ahead, with this goal in mind, I strive toward the prize of the upward call of God in Christ Jesus." (NET Bible) What is our mental perspective to be based on this verse?

_____

_____

_____

_____

_____

➢ Reflect and express what God just revealed to you.

_____

_____

_____

_____

_____

Day 5:

➢ Take a moment to pray. Tell God that you know He is willing to speak, but you want to be willing to hear what He says to you today and every day. (James 1:5)
➢ Read the devotion again.
➢ We all have gotten news that we did not want to receive. Write out Psalm 112:7 and 1 Peter 5:7 below. What are we supposed to do with our worries and cares?

_____

_____

_____

_____

_____

➤ Reflect and express what God just revealed to you.

_____

_____

_____

_____

_____

DAY 6

➤ Take a moment to pray, then read the devotion again.

➤ Read Job 33:4 and Psalm 146:2. How do these verses relate to "God has given me breath to live, to praise, to cry, to moan in anguish, but the focus in all my breathing has to remain constant and steady on the One who gave me breath?"

_____

_____

_____

_____

_____

➤ Reflect and express what God just revealed to you.

_____

_____

_____

_____

_____

DAY 7:

➢ Take a moment to pray. Tell God that you know He is willing to speak, but you want to be willing to hear what He says to you today and every day. (James 1:5)

➢ Read the devotion again.

➢ Read Days 1-6 again in their entirety.

➢ Reflect on the past days and express below what God has revealed to you.

_____

_____

_____

_____

_____

Creative Expressions

WEEK FIFTEEN
LESSONS IN THE BURDENS

It has been a long, hard season.

There should have been more tears.

There should have been more weeping, but I was being strong.

Unfortunately, I was being too strong, and that kind of strength comes with a price. When the weight is heavy relief must come soon and often, or you will break.

I never released the weight. I never release any of the weights. The new burdens get piled upon the old burdens. Some burdens have been around so long that they have begun to feel like me and smell like me. It is exceedingly difficult to detach yourself from what appears to be yourself, and it is exceedingly difficult to hold up well under all those burdens.

There must be a release.

Stuffing is a quick and relatively painless process, and it appears to provide great relief, for a season or two. Tears were meant to be a release valve but when a few feeble tears appeared, I instinctively shut them down. I cannot allow them to stay. Tears tend to run out of control, or worse yet, their arrival is an indicator that I should feel pain.

I don't want to feel pain.

I don't want to cry.

I want to feel success.

I want to run unhindered.

I want to be successful.

I don't want to feel pain.

Yet, here I am, at the end of many years of bearing unnecessary burdens, discovering that I no longer even know how to cry. The dead weight of the motionless burdens has permeated my entire being, and my entire being responds likewise, weighted down and motionless. Even my tears have learned that there is a line in the sand that they cannot cross. They may tiptoe to the precipice, but they do not have access to my skin. My face bears no tear tracks.

When others are hurting and grieving, I find myself stiff and motionless. I cannot both think rationally and feel their pain. Logic must win because they do not know how to move past their emotional state and think clearly enough to break free. I must help them find a way out and my tears get in the way. I cannot both feel the depth of their pain and navigate the course ahead.

But I'm tired of the desert.

I'm tired of the deadness.

I'm ready to feel again.

I want the tears to flow until the terrain of on my face is a river, not a desert. I want the tears to revive and release the pain. I want to release the burdens. I want to release the weight so I can inhale, so I can exhale, so I can rest, so I can process my life. I want to release the weight so I can feel joy again as well. It is such a joy to have joy uncovered after it's been buried.

> *"Those who plant in tears will harvest with shouts of joy. They weep as they go to plant their seed, but they sing as they return with the harvest." Psalm 126:5-6 (NLT)*

Thank you, Lord for the burdens.

Thank You for the pain.

Thank You for the desert.

Thank You for the lessons.

Thank You for the joy.

DAILY TIME WITH GOD

Day 1:

➢ Take a moment to pray. Tell God that you know He is willing to speak, but you want to be willing to hear what He says to you today and every day. (James 1:5)

➢ Read the devotion again.

➢ How would you describe the season you are in now? Is it a season of positive or negative emotions?

_____

_____

_____

_____

_____

➢ Are you feeling that you must be strong for someone else? Is there someone that you can contact to help you with this burden? Make a point to contact them in the next couple of days. I will ask you again later if you made this contact. Let God direct your conversation, but make sure you talk to them about your heavy load. Pray and talk to God about this burden first. Make any notes you want or write scripture(s) below.

_____

_____

_____

_____

_____

DAY 2:

➤ Take a moment to pray. Thank Him for Godly relationships in your life.

➤ Read the devotion again.

➤ Burdens are heavy loads, and heavy loads are not meant to be carried for long periods of time. How do you recognize the signs that you have exceeded your "weight limit" regarding holding onto old burdens? These God given signs are designed to help you recognize a problem. These signs can be emotional, physical, or spiritual. For me, my shoulders get tense, my breathing gets shallow, my thoughts are scattered, my emotions are irritable, and sitting to pray or read my Bible is usually a very distant thought.

_____

_____

_____

_____

_____

➤ Reflect and express what God just revealed to you.

_____

_____

_____

_____

DAY 3:

➤ Take a moment to pray using James 1:5 as your guide.

➤ Read the devotion again.

➤ As an occupational therapist, I work with both physical and emotional problems. You really cannot separate the physical and emotional. Each has a great impact on the other. Many times, people have lived with physical or emotional pain so long that they do not even recognize that it is there. They do not hear the irritability in their voice, or they do not see the elevated, tense shoulders.

➤ After you pray, ask God if He would allow you to openly ask a trusted Godly friend to tell you how they feel you are managing life's burdens. Ask God to allow the Holy Spirit to speak through their words to correct you and to lovingly point you back in the right direction. Remember, God's goal in showing you the error of your ways is not to shame you but to release you. He is always looking to set the captives free! "The Spirit of the Lord GOD is upon me, because the LORD has anointed me to bring good news to the poor; he has sent me to bind up the brokenhearted, to proclaim liberty to the captives, and the opening of the prison to those who are bound." Isaiah 61:1 (ESV)

➤ Reflect and express what God is saying to you.

_____

_____

_____

_____

_____

DAY 4:

➤ Take a moment to pray, then read the devotion again.

➤ What are healthy ways to release burdens? Journaling, crying, exercising, deep breathing, walking, and sitting outside are great to help with the pressure from the burdens. God has designed a way to help with heavy burdens. "Bear one another's burdens, and so fulfill the law of Christ." Galatians 6:2 (ESV) Practically, what does that mean to you as a load bearer? Also, practically, what does that mean to you as one who has a friend with a heavy load?

➤ When someone is in a season of life when there is a heavy load, I will tell to call me any time day or night. I have learned that most will not, so I go a step further and ask the question that they were not expecting: "If I were in a rough situation, would you want me to call you anytime if I really needed someone to talk to?" They begrudgingly agree. Isn't it ironic that we would love to be available for someone, but when we are on the other end of the "needy stick," we isolate and do not follow the Biblical mandate to let other's share our burdens? Have you done this? Write out a declaration prayer to God asking Him to allow you to humbly ask for help, knowing that it is not a sign of weakness but a sign of obedience. By the way, have you contacted that trusted friend yet?

_____

_____

_____

_____

_____

DAY 5:

➤ Take a moment to pray. Tell God that you are thankful that He is available any time day or night.

➤ Read the devotion again.

➤ Are you a problem solver for others? Have you, through these devotions and reflections this week noticed that you cannot "both feel the depth of their pain and navigate the course ahead?" Or do you sit and cry with them? I think there needs to be a healthy dose of both responses. People need compassion and if you are also able to help them navigate the road ahead, then do both. Compassion is at the heart of God and wisdom is promised when we ask (James 1:5). Ask God to show you how to balance both responses with a listening ear for any instructions He may give you for your friend. If instructions do not come, then your presence is what is needed most. I find that my relationship with God is the same way at times. When a situation is overwhelming, I just want to feel His presence. Answers may not come, but His presence is solace to my tattered soul. Talk to Him now. If He leads, write what He says.

_____

_____

_____

_____

_____

DAY 6

➤ Take a moment to pray. Tell God that you know He is willing to speak, but you want to be willing to hear what He says to you today and every day. (James 1:5)

➤ Read the devotion again.

➤ Can you thank Him for the desert? Can you thank Him for the lessons? Joy comes in the morning, my friend. Thank Him for it all.

_____

_____

_____

_____

_____

DAY 7:

➢ Take a moment to pray, then read the devotion again.

➢ Read Days 1-6 again in their entirety.

➢ Reflect on the past days and express below what God has revealed to you.

_____

_____

_____

_____

_____

Creative Expressions

THE PONDERING PERSON

Having established the fact that you were created to ponder, and specifically to ponder God, it stands to reason that the enemy will do anything to keep you from your created purpose. He does not want you to spend any amount of time with God much less stepping out of the intellectual arena and peacefully reposing with Him. Satan wants you too busy to do what matters most—spending time with your heavenly Father. Yet, you were created for this.

Think of Mary, sitting at the feet of Jesus.

Think of David under a star filled sky.

Think of Jesus awakening early to be with the Father.

Think of you, pulling out of the steady demands of the day to be still in His presence.

Stop for a moment right now and purposefully focus on your breathing. Close your eyes and take a few deep breaths. Imagine having unhurried time with the One who loves you most. When you open your eyes, close them again and just keep breathing and envisioning for a few more moments.

This is the essence of pondering – restful repose; relaxation; recumbent in your mind. Your body is peaceful while your mind casually engages with the Creator.

> *"How amazing are the deeds of the LORD! All who delight in him should **ponder** them. Everything he does reveals his glory and majesty. His righteousness never fails. He causes us to remember his wonderful works. How gracious and merciful is our LORD!"* Psalm 111:2-4 (ESV, emphasis mine)

I want to be like Mary, sitting at the feet of Jesus.

I want to be like David, a man after God's own heart.

I want to be like Jesus, intentional with my time and focus.

I want to be a ponderer at heart.

CHANGE

Therefore, if anyone is in Christ, he is a new creation. The old has passed away; behold, the new has come.

2 Corinthians 5:17 (ESV)

WIRED FOR CHANGE

I am fascinated by the fact that God has wired us with the ability to change.

That fact alone is a game changer.

You are not stuck where you are.

If you feel that you are not in a good place, do not worry. You have yet to find the way out of your current thinking pattern, but do not worry about that either; God has a plan.

God has wired us for perfection; however, when a traumatic or stressful event happens, the enemy offers a belief about that situation. Although it may make sense at the time, he is the father of lies; therefore, his logical offer is actually a destructive belief system or thought pattern which forms a seemingly hopeless mental picture. Soon that belief system becomes a stronghold from which he offers similar information to keep us believing his lies. We become encased in walls of lies. Wall upon wall begins to form a formative stronghold, and before we realize it, we have become captive to his lies.

Thankfully, you are not hopelessly lost inside the walls. God has a plan. God has always had a plan for all that you experience in life.

God says to meditate on His word. When His words are firmly rooted in your mind, then you can instantly reject anything contradictory to His words. During those days when you are planting His truth in your mind, know that there will be times when you feel like you do not know enough, but the Holy Spirit living inside of you can guide you perfectly without you knowing the whole Bible. Trust Him.

Surround yourself with people who see everything from God's perspective and speak His truth into every situation. You will learn how to handle life in a Godly manner from those who consistently handle life in this way. God made us for relationship and community so find a trustworthy, Godly friend or two who you can do life with.

If a wrong thought pattern has already formed, repair the relationship with the Heavenly Father by confessing your unbelief in Him, and confess your alliance with the father of lies. Immediately begin filling your mind and your voice with God's words (Romans 12:1-2). for although the Bible talks about stopping things, the victorious focus is on what to do instead. If we do not actively replace the negative actions or mindsets, the old returns and that reinforces the mindset that change is impossible. With God, all things are possible.

Play worship songs and sing out loud so you can fill the air around you with the good news of God's love and grace. The enemy hates those songs. Sing loud. Sing confidently, for you are forgiven and you are loved.

You can connect with a friend and ask them for prayer and accountability. True Godly friends encourage you when you have fallen. Restoration is at the heart of God, and it should be in our friends' hearts as well.

Erroneous thought patterns will be offered by the enemy again, for he does not like to lose. Run from those thoughts like they are the plague. There may be morsels of truth in them, but they also contain morsels of poison, and no one wants any amount of poison in their mind. You are not responsible for the lies the enemy throws at you, but you are responsible for not "taking up the shield of faith with which you will be able to extinguish all the flaming arrows of the evil one." Ephesians 6:16 (ESV)

You are not stuck where you are. You can be victorious.

God has a plan for that.

God has a plan for you.

DAILY TIME WITH GOD:

DAY 1:

➢ Take a moment to pray. Tell God that you know He is willing to speak, but you want to be willing to hear what He says to you today and every day. (James 1:5)

➢ Read the devotion again.

➢ God has wired us to be able to change. What does that mean to you? What does that say about His plans for you and His love for you?

_____

_____

_____

_____

DAY 2:

➢ Take a moment to pray. Thank Him for the way He created us.

➢ Read the devotion again.

➢ Take a moment and evaluate your current thinking pattern. Is it an optimistic or pessimistic outlook? Is it cynical or hopeful? Is it problem centered, or solution centered? Reflect and express what God just revealed to you.

_____

_____

_____

_____

DAY 3:

➢ Take a moment to pray and ask Him to renew your mind during this time.

➢ Read the devotion again.

➢ 'The enemy offers a belief system' about a situation. He does not sit idly by and let any opportunity pass to try to get you to question or doubt God. He wants you to hear his nuggets of information. He wants you to hear him first. He wants to be the sound closest to your ear. Do you listen? Do you entertain his thoughts? Many of us do, and then that becomes our default reaction, which in turn becomes a pattern of thinking that is contradictory to God's words. Ponder and pray about the voice that you listen to the most. Confess to God what He brings to your mind. If He leads, journal about it or express it in the margin.

_____

_____

_____

_____

_____

DAY 4:

➢ Take a moment to pray. Tell God that you know He is willing to speak, but you want to be willing to hear what He says to you today and every day. (James 1:5)
➢ Read the devotion again.
➢ I have heard that bank tellers are taught to recognize counterfeit money, but probably not in the way you would think. Instead of having them study them counterfeit bills, there were told to intensely study the originals instead. By doing this, the bank tellers could instantly recognize anything that deviated from the real thing. The same is true with our thought life. If we spend time in His word, then anything that contradicts it can be immediately rejected as lies. This is why you want to continuously read His word. Talk to God about this. If God leads you, write what He tells you.

_____

_____

_____

_____

DAY 5:

➤ Take a moment to pray. Thank Him for the guidance from His Word.

➤ Read the devotion again.

➤ "Surround yourself with people who see everything from God's perspective and speak His truth into every situation. You will learn how to handle life in a Godly manner from those who consistently handle life in this way. God made us for relationship and community so find a trustworthy, Godly friend or two who you can do life with."

Have you ever thought that friends can help to keep your thoughts God centered? God made us for relationship and community. We can show others the way to Him, but we also can be the recipient of Godly wisdom from Godly relationships. I have greatly benefitted from being around those who enter every conversation with a Godly point of view. They have impacted my life and my kingdom purposes more than they may ever know in this life.

➤ Do you surround yourself with God centered people? Do you watch how they respond and feel the impact it makes on you and your life? Take some time to thank God if you have those people in your life. If you do not, take some time to ask Him to send those people to you or make you aware of where they are in your life.

_____

_____

_____

_____

_____

DAY 6

➤ Take a moment to pray using James 1:5 as your guide.

➤ Read the devotion again.

➤ Fill your mind and your voice with God's word. Sing out loud. The enemy hates songs of God's love and grace. Do you really understand His love and grace yourself? It is not going to be easy to convince an enemy that he does not have the victory if you do not believe you have the victory either. You are made for victory, and you are made to change. When you have fallen into a pattern of erroneous thinking from the enemy, confess and relish in God's love and grace. He loves you. He loves you. He loves you. Nothing can change His love for you.

➤ Consider this scripture on grace:
"And God is able to make every grace overflow to you, so that in every way, always having everything you need, you may excel in every good work." 1 Corinthians 9:8 (HCSB)

➤ Let's take another moment to soak up more truth from His word. "No, in all these things we are more than conquerors through him who loved us. For I am convinced that neither death nor life, neither angels nor demons, neither the present nor the future, nor any powers, neither height nor depth, nor anything else in all creation, will be able to separate us from the love of God that is in Christ Jesus our Lord." Romans 8:37-39 (NIV)

➤ Reflect and express what God just revealed to you.

_____

_____

_____

_____

_____

DAY 7:

➤ Take a moment to pray. Tell God that you know He is willing to speak, but you want to be willing to hear what He says to you today and every day. (James 1:5)

➤ Read the devotion again.

➤ Read Days 1-6 again in their entirety.

➤ Reflect on the past days and express below what God has revealed to you.

_____

_____

_____

_____

_____

Creative Expressions

CHANGING WHAT WE SPEAK

Have you ever said things like this?

"I hope that this doesn't go that way."
"I hope you get what you asked for."
"I hope that doesn't happen to you."
"I hope it stays sunny all day."

Even though the word *hope* is used in those sentences, there doesn't seem to be much hope in things turning out the way that we want. It seems like hope is being referred in such a hopeless way. Using *hope* in such a doubtful way makes neither the hearer nor the speaker feel any more hopeful after the words are said.

I have said those sentences far more times than I care to admit. As I began to realize how empty my "hope filled" words were, I did not like it, but I did not know how to change those words. I had said them for as long as I could remember, and they seemed like the right words to use. It is hard to explain how attached I was to empty words.

Unfortunately, I found myself floundering on what to say instead of, "I hope." When you say something for years and years without really thinking about it, it becomes part of you. One day, I had the brilliant idea to replace the "I hope" phrase with a more spiritual phrase, "I will pray that _____." Saying "I will pray" sounded so much better than "I hope." I truly had good intentions to pray for that person or that situation, but the normal issues of life crowded in very quickly and I forgot to pray for them. My new words did not change the outcome. When you throw a praying phrase around (action) without actually praying (inaction), not only did you *not* contribute to hope but you then *added* lying as the only action you actually did. Obviously, I needed another solution.

Then one day I came across this statement while reading a commentary on 2 Thessalonians 3:16:

"...loving wishes are potent when they are changed into petitions" (Maclaren Expositions).

This statement summarized why I was feeling discontent with the "I hope" statements, but it also made me realize that I needed to follow through on my praying statements. Changing my wording was not the solution, praying was. Instead of telling people that I would pray for them and then forgetting to do it, I began to ask people if I could pray with them at the very moment they asked for prayer or expressed hopelessness about a situation. This simple action broke the powerless words and changed those words into loving petitions that brought hope because we brought them to the God of hope.

God wants us to be effective with our words and our actions. He wants us to point others to Him as the source of change instead of offering vague and empty statements devoid of power.

Hoping for change makes us feel like victims to the winds of fate.

We are not victims.

We are more than conquerors through Him that loves us.

We need to be mindful of our words, for words are important.

We need to be careful of leading ourselves and others into agreeing with hopelessness.

Step into action and speak life.

Praying for change changes things.

Let the Holy Spirit empower your words and lead people into a relationship with the Author of Hope and the power to change lives, situations and even our hopeless words.

DAILY TIME WITH GOD

DAY 1:

➤ Take a moment to pray. Tell God that you know He is willing to speak, but you want to be willing to hear what He says to you today and every day. (James 1:5)

➤ Read the devotion again.

➤ Have you ever heard yourself telling someone that you hope something will change? Did it make you feel powerful or powerless?

_____

_____

_____

_____

_____

➤ Write out a prayer asking God to let you know when you speak powerless words like "I hope" and to give you the ability to lead yourself or another person to the throne room to make your petitions known.

_____

_____

_____

_____

_____

DAY 2:

➤ Take a moment to pray. Thank Him for giving you power. Ask Him to teach you more about that power.

➤ Read the devotion again.

➤ Write out 2 Thessalonians 3:16.

_____

_____

_____

_____

_____

➤ Reflect and express what God just revealed to you.

_____

_____

_____

_____

DAY 3:

➤ Take a moment to pray, then read the devotion again.
➤ Write out Romans 8:37. What hope do you find in this verse?

_____

_____

_____

_____

➤ Reflect and express what God is saying to you:

_____

_____

_____

_____

DAY 4:

- ➤ Take time to thank Him for whatever comes to your mind today.
- ➤ Pray, then read the devotion again.
- ➤ Write out Romans 8:38-39. What hope do we find in these verses?

_____

_____

_____

_____

_____

- ➤ Reflect and express what God just revealed to you.

_____

_____

_____

_____

_____

DAY 5:

- ➤ Take a moment to pray using James 1:5 as your guide.
- ➤ Read the devotion again.
- ➤ Write out Jeremiah 29:11-13. When you learn that God has plans for you, you are supposed to do what? And what will you find?

_____

_____

_____

_____

_____

➤ Reflect and express what God just revealed to you.

_____

_____

_____

_____

_____

DAY 6

➤ Take a moment to pray. Thank God for His plans for you.

➤ Read the devotion again.

➤ Write out Proverbs 18:21. What does it say is in the power of our words (tongue)? What does that mean to you?

_____

_____

_____

_____

_____

➤ Reflect and express what God just revealed to you through your answers.

_____

_____

_____

_____

_____

DAY 7:

- ➢ Take a moment to pray. Tell God that you know He is willing to speak, but you want to be willing to hear what He says to you today and every day. (James 1:5)
- ➢ Read the devotion again.
- ➢ Read Days 1-6 again in their entirety.
- ➢ Reflect on the past days and express below what God has revealed to you.

_____

_____

_____

_____

_____

Creative Expressions

OUR WAYWARD THOUGHTS

Training our wayward thoughts to obey Christ is imperative.

When you fail to take your thoughts captive to the obedience of Christ, the consequences can be detrimental. Wayward thoughts can lead to wayward actions. Wayward thoughts can lead to a wayward mindset. Fear is not from God. Fear looks like and acts like the opposite of God, so why do we allow those wayward thoughts in the first place?

I believe it comes down to the root of all sin…pride. We pride ourselves on being in control rather than being teachable. Satan convinces us that being teachable will make us look less capable and less intelligent. However, constantly searching to find the answers so that you can remain in control is exhausting. It will quickly deplete you. It will quickly steal your joy. Plus, when you are trying to be in control and others do not cooperate with your plan, great discord will usually arise. This is not glorifying to Him.

Release.

Let God be God and allow Him to run the show. This is humbling but it is effective. It starts by taking your thoughts captive to the obedience of Christ.

Training your wayward thoughts to obey Christ is imperative.

You are not in control. You are not the Master. You are the student. Students live under the master's control. As the student, you are allowed to not know everything.

We are in the student's role here on earth. We can be wrong at times, but we have a Heavenly Father who forgives us and asks us to walk in reconciliation with Him and our fellow man.

We are not knowledgeable in all subjects, but we have a God who knows everything and promises to give us wisdom when we ask.

We have imperfections, with a Savior who picks us up, cleans us up, and points us in the right direction.

From the position of our last mistake is the next step toward fulfillment, the next breath for thankfulness and the necessary energy for Kingdom purposes.

Train your thoughts. Release those fears. Walk in power.

Take your thoughts captive to the obedience of Christ.

Stay your mind on Him and He will keep you in perfect peace.

"I have said these things to you, that in me you may have peace. In the world you will have tribulation. But take heart; I have overcome the world." John 16:33 (ESV)

DAILY TIME WITH GOD

DAY 1:

➢ Take a moment to pray. Tell God that you know He is willing to speak, but you want to be willing to hear what He says to you today and every day. (James 1:5)
➢ Read the devotion again.
➢ "We destroy arguments and every lofty opinion raised against the knowledge of God, and take every thought captive to obey Christ." (2 Corinthians 10:5, ESV) Why is it imperative to train our wayward thoughts to obey Christ?

_____

_____

_____

_____

_____

➤ Reflect and express what God has shown you:

_____

_____

_____

_____

_____

DAY 2:

➤ Take a moment to pray, then read the devotion again.
➤ How do wayward thoughts lead to wayward actions?

_____

_____

_____

_____

_____

➤ Reflect and express what God just revealed to you.

_____

_____

_____

_____

_____

DAY 3:

➤ Take a moment to pray. Thank Him for His presence, for His presence is what we need.
➤ Read the devotion again.
➤ Do you feel that if you are not in control, you look less capable or less intelligent? What does letting go of control and being teachable look like in your life?

_____

_____

_____

_____

_____

➢ Reflect and express what God has shown you:

_____

_____

_____

_____

DAY 4:

➢ Take a moment to pray. Thank Him that He is trustworthy.
➢ Read the devotion again.
➢ Are you constantly trying to find answers and solutions to your problems yourself? Is it exhausting? Is it causing discord between you and others? Think about those answers and reflect and express what God has shown you:

_____

_____

_____

_____

DAY 5:

➢ Take a moment to pray using James 1:5 as your guide.
➢ Read the devotion again.

➤ Take time to look up the definition of a student and write it down. Could you be called a student of God after looking up this definition? Write out a prayer devoting yourself to becoming a true student of God.

_____

_____

_____

_____

_____

Reflect and express what God has shown you:

_____

_____

_____

_____

DAY 6:

➤ Don't forget to take time to pray. It does not need to be long; it just needs to be done.
➤ Read the devotion again.
➤ From the devotion, write out what we have when we are wrong at times, when we are not knowledgeable in all subjects, and when we are imperfect. I have started the first part of each sentence for you.

When I am wrong, I have…

_____

_____

_____

_____

_____

When I am not knowledgeable in all subjects, I have…

_____

_____

_____

_____

I am imperfect, but I have…

_____

_____

_____

_____

➤ Next, write out what should you do or say or whatever action you feel called to focus on after the next mistake you make.

_____

_____

_____

_____

➤ Reflect and express what God has shown you:

_____

_____

_____

_____

_____

DAY 7:

➤ Take a moment to pray. Tell God that you know He is willing to speak, but you want to be willing to hear what He says to you today and every day. (James 1:5)

➤ Read the devotion again.

➤ Read Days 1-6 again in their entirety.

➤ Reflect on the past days and express below what God has revealed to you.

_____

_____

_____

_____

_____

Creative Expressions

GRACE

For sin will have no dominion over you, since you are not under law but under grace.

Romans 6:14 (ESV)

WEEK NINETEEN
IT'S ALL ABOUT GRACE

Grace.

The word stands out from all the rest the words on the page of my Bible.

Those who have not tasted grace feel buried alive from the weight of the world.

Those who have tasted grace realize that we are not of this world; therefore, we cannot be buried underneath the weight of this world for we are seated in heavenly places. I am seated in heavenly places. I have traded the weight of the world for the God of all creation.

It is all about relationship.

It is all about grace.

It is all about His love for me and my love for Him.

It is a simple plan for life...

Love God.

Love people.

It is all about relationship.

It is all about grace.

DAILY TIME WITH GOD

DAY 1:

➤ Take a moment to pray. Tell God that you know He is willing to speak, but you want to be willing to hear what He says to you today and every day. (James 1:5)

➤ Read the devotion again.

➤ Take time to look up the definition of grace and write it out below. Take a moment and express what God shows you.

_____

_____

_____

_____

_____

DAY 2:

➤ Take a moment to pray. This should be such a sweet time of communion with Him. Sometimes, you don't even have to use words. Just take a moment to sit with Him during your prayer time today.

➤ Read the devotion again.

➤ Ephesians 2:8-9 says, "For by grace you have been saved through faith. And this is not your own doing; it is the gift of God, not a result of works, so that no one may boast." (ESV)

Hebrews 4:16 says, "Let us then with confidence draw near to the throne of grace, that we may receive mercy and find grace to help in time of need." (ESV)

Does grace sound different than any other word you know? Why? Does the word grace stand out on the pages of your Bible?

_____

_____

_____

_____

_____

➤ Reflect and express what God has shown you:

_____

_____

_____

_____

DAY 3:

➤ Take a moment to pray, then read the devotion again.

➤ "And you were dead in the trespasses and sins in which you once walked, following the course of this world, following the prince of the power of the air, the spirit that is now at work in the sons of disobedience— among whom we all once lived in the passions of our flesh, carrying out the desires of the body and the mind, and were by nature children of wrath, like the rest of mankind. But God, being rich in mercy, because of the great love with which he loved us, even when we were dead in our trespasses, made us alive together with Christ—by grace you have been saved..." (Ephesians 2:1-22, ESV)

➤ You are not of this world. What does this statement mean to you regarding the cares of this world?

_____

_____

_____

_____

➤ Reflect and express what God has shown you:

_____

_____

_____

_____

DAY 4:

➢ Take a moment to pray using James 1:5 as your guide.

➢ Read the devotion again.

➢ Titus 2:11-14 talks about our relationship to Him and His grace which brought that about, "For the grace of God has appeared, bringing salvation for all people, training us to renounce ungodliness and worldly passions, and to live self-controlled, upright, and godly lives in the present age, waiting for our blessed hope, the appearing of the glory of our great God and Savior Jesus Christ, who gave himself for us to redeem us from all lawlessness, and to purify for himself a people for his own possession who are zealous for good works." (ESV)

➢ Take some time to thank Him for relationship and for grace.

_____

_____

_____

_____

_____

DAY 5:

➢ Take a moment to pray. Tell God how amazing it is that He would want to spend time with us then read the devotion again.

➢ "It is a simple plan for life. Love God. Love people."
Is life this simple? Was it this simple for Jesus? Did He model this for us? Let's look at John 1:14 (ESV): "And the Word became flesh and dwelt among us, and we have seen his glory, glory as of the only Son from the Father, full of grace and truth." And Colossians 4:2-6 (ESV): "Continue steadfastly in prayer, being watchful in it with thanksgiving. At the same time, pray also for us, that God may open to us a door for the word, to declare the mystery of Christ, on account of which I am in prison—that I may make it clear, which is how I ought to speak. Walk in wisdom toward outsiders, making the best use of the time. Let your speech always be gracious, seasoned with salt, so that you may know how you ought to answer each person."

➤ Reflect and express what God has shown you:

_____

_____

_____

_____

_____

DAY 6

➤ Take a moment to pray. Tell God that you know He is willing to speak, but you want to be willing to hear what He says to you today and every day. (James 1:5)

➤ Read the devotion again.

➤ Read over these scriptures:

"The LORD bless you and keep you; the LORD make his face to shine upon you and be gracious to you; the LORD lift up his countenance upon you and give you peace." Numbers 6:24-26 (ESV)

"For God so loved the world, that he gave his only Son, that whoever believes in him should not perish but have eternal life." John 3:16 (ESV)

"And God is able to make all grace abound to you, so that having all sufficiency in all things at all times, you may abound in every good work." 2 Corinthians 9:8 (ESV)

These are just a few references to the goodness and grace of God. Spend time thanking Him for His goodness. Spend time thanking Him for His grace.

_____

_____

_____

_____

DAY 7:

➤ Take a moment to pray, then read the devotion again.

➤ Read Days 1-6 again in their entirety.

➤ Reflect on the past days and express below what God has revealed to you.

_____

_____

_____

_____

_____

Creative Expressions

YOUR HEART'S AFFECTIONS

"Thus Jehoshaphat reigned over Judah. He was thirty-five years old when he began to reign, and he reigned twenty-five years in Jerusalem. His mother's name was Azubah the daughter of Shilhi. He walked in the way of Asa his father and did not turn aside from it, doing what was right in the sight of the LORD. The high places, however, were not taken away; the people had not yet set their hearts upon the God of their fathers." 2 Chronicles 20:31-33 (ESV)

Those last two sentences...He was doing what was right in the sight of the LORD; however, the high places were not taken away and hearts were not set upon the God of their fathers.

Doing right—but having high places (ungodly affections)—and a heart not devoted to God.

How many times do we fit this description? I long for a day when my heart's affection is not fickle to the things of this world. I strive in my devotion to Him, but this world pulls at me more than I care to admit.

I take comfort in knowing that the great apostle Paul had the same dilemma. In Romans 7, he says:

"So I find it to be a law that when I want to do right, evil lies close at hand. For I delight in the law of God, in my inner being, but I see in my members another law waging war against the law of my mind and making me captive to the law of sin that dwells in my members. Wretched man that I am! Who will deliver me from this body of death? Thanks be to God through Jesus Christ our Lord! So then, I myself serve the law of God with my mind, but with my flesh I serve the law of sin." (verses 21-25, ESV)

But in Romans 8, he breaks forth with the solace of my soul... (you should read the whole chapter. It's that good!)

"For God has done what the law, weakened by the flesh, could not do. By sending his own Son in the likeness of sinful flesh and for sin, he condemned sin in the flesh, in order that the righteous requirement of the law might be fulfilled in us, who walk not according to the flesh but according to the Spirit." (verses 3-4, ESV)

"Likewise the Spirit helps us in our weakness. For we do not know what to pray for as we ought, but the Spirit himself intercedes for us with groanings too deep for words. And he who searches hearts knows what is the mind of the Spirit, because the Spirit intercedes for the saints according to the will of God." (verses 26-27, ESV)

"No, in all these things we are more than conquerors through him who loved us. For I am sure that neither death nor life, nor angels nor rulers, nor things present nor things to come, nor powers, nor height nor depth, nor anything else in all creation, will be able to separate us from the love of God in Christ Jesus our Lord." (verses 37-39, ESV)

Yes, sometimes I feel like I am stuck in Romans 7....

"For I do not understand my own actions. For I do not do what I want, but I do the very thing I hate." (verse 15, ESV)

But a wise pastor responded to my dilemma by saying, "Maybe turn the page and live in, soak up, and claim Romans 8"[9]

I am so thankful that as I rise every morning, I find mercy. I find comfort in knowing that even though I am striving to please Him in this mortal body that has desires of its own, I am still His...holy and beloved, blessed by God, the apple of His eye, a child of the king...flawed but blessed and grateful beyond measure!

Go in peace knowing that He does not require your perfection, but He does desire your heart's devotion. You can give Him that, and that is pleasing to Him.

DAILY TIME WITH GOD

DAY 1:

➢ Take a moment to pray. Tell God that you know He is willing to speak, but you want to be willing to hear what He says to you today and every day. (James 1:5)

➢ Read the devotion again.

➢ A heart not devoted to God, and the high places (ungodly affections) were still standing. How many times do you fit this description? Do you long to have a heart that is devoted to Him? Do you long for the day when the cares of this world do not pull you away from His continual presence?

➢ Take time to ponder the state of your heart. Are there any "high places" that need to come down? Sit in His presence and ask Him to speak. Express what He says if He so leads.

_____

_____

_____

_____

_____

DAY 2:

➢ Take a moment to pray. Ponder His presence. What does it feel like to sit with Him?

➢ Read the devotion again.

➢ Is it new to you to realize that the great apostle Paul had the same dilemma of wanting to do what was right, but he did not do it, as well the struggle of not doing the things he wanted to do? Why do you think God allowed Paul to share his dilemma with us? For me, it makes me realize that I am not alone in my struggles. How does it make you feel? As you write, remember that condemnation is not of God. You are still loved when you fail—Paul was.

_____

_____

_____

_____

_____

Day 3:

➤ Take a moment to pray using James 1:5 as your guide.

➤ Read the devotion again.

➤ Have you ever realized that Chapter 8 of Romans makes a 180 degree turn from the futile attempts of man to the effective and all-encompassing power of God through Jesus Christ? (it actually begins to make this turn in the final verse of chapter 7). Read Romans 8 if you have time and let God's all-encompassing and effective power resonate with every cell of your body.

➤ Reflect and express what God is saying to you.

_____

_____

_____

_____

Day 4:

➤ Take a moment to pray. Thank Him for the ability to make a 180 degree turn in our lives.

➤ Read the devotion again.

➤ All too often we focus on our failures, but can you say this about yourself out loud with conviction: I am "holy and beloved, blessed by God, the apple of His eye, a child of the king...flawed but blessed?" Do you see yourself that way or do you see yourself as the sum of your failures? Talk to God about how He wants you to see you.

Reflect and express what God just revealed to you.

_____

_____

_____

_____

_____

DAY 5:

➤ Take a moment to pray, then read the devotion again.

➤ For the last couple of days, we looked at who you are in Christ as we "turned the page" from Chapter 7 of Romans. I loved my pastor's response, "Maybe turn the page and live in, soak up, and claim Romans 8" but honestly, I only remember the first part, "turn the page." He was so right. God does not want us to live in Romans 7. We may have days in which we act like we are in Romans 7; but that is not our home, and therefore, that should not be our mindset. Talk to God about your mindset and His desires for you to be victorious through His Son.

_____

_____

_____

_____

DAY 6

➤ Take a moment to pray. Thank Him for presence again. I feel like we should recognize the importance of His presence.

➤ Read the devotion again.

➤ How good are you at giving yourself grace when you mess up (Romans 7)? Can you say this to yourself: "Go in peace today knowing that He does not require your mortal perfection for that is impossible, but He does greatly desire your heart's devotion, for that is possible. Set your heart on Him, turn the page, and gratefully walk in grace."

➤ Spend time focusing on those words above and hear His love for you, even with your flaws and failures.

_____

_____

_____

_____

_____

DAY 7:

➤ Take a moment to pray. Tell God that you know He is willing to speak, but you want to be willing to hear what He says to you today and every day. (James 1:5)

➤ Read the devotion again.

➤ Read Days 1-6 again in their entirety.

➤ Reflect on the past days and express below what God has revealed to you.

_____

_____

_____

_____

_____

Creative Expressions

PROTECTION AND PROVISION

"The LORD will guide you always; he will satisfy your needs in a sun-scorched land and will strengthen your frame. You will be like a well-watered garden, like a spring whose waters never fail." (Isaiah 58:11, NIV)

As I was reading my Bible one morning, this scripture seemed more amazing than I had ever noticed before. I just sat back and marveled at how peaceful I felt in His provision. It wasn't monetary provisions, but security and well-being, satisfaction and guidance. If you have had a father or a husband who is a strong leader, who provides, protects and guides you, then you feel loved, cared for and secure. The Father is promising all of that to us and so much more, for He Himself is guiding, providing, and strengthening us.

Let's read that scripture again and this time picture yourself being the recipient of His attentive care.

"The LORD will guide you always; he will satisfy your needs in a sun-scorched land and will strengthen your frame. You will be like a well-watered garden, like a spring whose waters never fail."

Guidance by God Himself.

Continual guidance.

Satisfaction in my soul.

Satisfaction in scorched places.

Strength to my bones.

A watered garden.

A spring of water.

An unfailing spring of water.

When I understand all that this verse is conveying to me, how can I not desire to be in His presence? How can I not realize His unfailing love?

Dear Lord, I just want to be in Your presence.

I just want to hear You speak.

I just want to be near to You.

DAILY TIME WITH GOD

DAY 1:

➤ Take a moment to pray. Tell God that you know He is willing to speak, but you want to be willing to hear what He says to you today and every day. (James 1:5)

➤ Read the devotion today again and pause and visualize each of these things one by one. Don't rush. Just let each word linger.
Guidance by God Himself.

Continual guidance.

Satisfaction in my soul.

Satisfaction in scorched places.

Strength to my bones.

A watered garden.

A spring of water.

An unfailing spring of water.

➤ Sit a little longer if needed. You may not even want to engage in the lines or margins today. You may just want to bask in what you just read. If you feel that God had revealed something to you that you want to remember, journal it or creatively express it.

_____

_____

_____

_____

_____

DAY 2:

➤ Take a moment to pray, then read the devotion again.
➤ What does it mean to receive guidance from God Himself?

_____

_____

_____

_____

_____

➤ What does it mean to have continual guidance? Do you accept continual guidance from Him?

_____

_____

_____

_____

_____

➤ Reflect and express what God just revealed to you:

_____

_____

_____

_____

DAY 3:

➤ Take a moment to pray. Thank Him for guidance.
➤ Read the devotion again.
➤ What does it mean to you to have your soul satisfied in scorched places?

_____

_____

_____

_____

_____

➤ Do you have any scorched places that you need to talk to Him about?

_____

_____

_____

_____

➤ Reflect and express what God just revealed to you:

_____

_____

_____

_____

DAY 4:

➤ Take a moment to pray using James 1:5 as a guide.

➤ Read the devotion again.

➤ What are your bones for physically? You do not need to have expertise in this area. What is the first thing you think of when you think of the reason God gave our bodies bones? (God likes it when we keep it simple, childlike simple).

_____

_____

_____

_____

_____

➤ Why would your bones need to be strengthened? If our bones in the physical world are to bear weight and give us stability and strength, and we need to strengthen them to walk, to move things in our environment, to carry loads, to carry our own body weight. Why would our bones need to be strengthened in the spiritual world?

If you can, write out your answer before you look at my thoughts below or use the blank spaces for creative expression.

_____

_____

_____

_____

_____

My thoughts: Maybe our bones need to be strengthened to provide the strength to stand, the strength to fight, stability against the dark forces, the ability to walk in the way He has called us to walk, and to bear the weight of our own work that He has called us to do.

➤ Reflect and express what God just revealed to you:

_____

_____

_____

_____

_____

DAY 5:

➤ Take a moment to pray. Make sure you give space in that prayer time to listen, even if it is just for a moment.

➤ Read the devotion again.

➤ What does a watered garden look like? Is there a difference in the image in your mind of a watered garden and a well-watered garden? Let's look at it another way, a garden that has just enough water to produce green foliage does not always have enough water to produce fruit.

➤ What does it mean for you to be compared to a well-watered garden? What fruit would you produce?

_____

_____

_____

_____

_____

➤ Reflect and express what God just revealed to you:

_____

_____

_____

_____

DAY 6:

➤ Take a moment to pray. Tell God that you know He is willing to speak, but you want to be willing to hear what He says to you today and every day. (James 1:5)

➤ Read the devotion again.

➤ What does a spring of water look like? Again, comparison sometimes helps us when trying to understand things. The writer could have said that you will be like water or a river, but he specifically used the phrase, "a spring of water." What does it mean that you will be like a "spring of water?"

_____

_____

_____

_____

_____

➤ What does it mean that your waters will not fail?

_____

_____

_____

_____

_____

➤ Reflect and express what God just revealed to you:

_____

_____

_____

_____

_____

DAY 7:

➢ Take a moment to pray. Thank Him for provision and protection.
➢ Read the devotion again.
➢ Read Days 1-6 again in their entirety.
➢ Reflect on it all and express below what God just showed you.

_____

_____

_____

_____

_____

Creative Expressions

THE PONDERING LIFESTYLE

··

In the beginning of this book, I stated that "you will grow at the skill of pondering and you will find His rhythm so you will be able to effortlessly move in and out of pondering at any time of the day. Who knows, maybe pondering will become the norm and chaotic will not find a place to lay its head. The enemy wants you busy. God wants you to 'be still and know.'"

Can you envision yourself walking in a lifestyle of pondering? Moving in and out of pondering at any time of the day, or night? There is a lifestyle that holds pondering in the core of its being. It is a lens that views everything in light of His presence and goodness. It hears Him in the silence. It reads between the lines. It turns aside and reconsiders what it just saw. It knows that God wants to communicate, but there will always be a need to be still.

For just a brief moment, let's look at something in Genesis 3:8:

> *"And they heard the sound of the LORD God walking in the garden in the cool of the day, and the man and his wife hid themselves from the presence of the LORD God among the trees of the garden." (ESV)*

Ponder this verse for a moment (i.e., reread this verse a couple of times). Did you catch that God was *walking* in the garden looking for Adam and Eve? Can you imagine what it was like to walk and talk with God? I bet it was not a fast-paced walk. I just cannot imagine God quickly showing Adam and Eve a bunch of stuff, giving them a list of things to do, then leaving. I do not sense a hurried boss wanting to tell His employees something. I envision a father wanting to explain the family business to his heirs. It takes time to tell all the ins and outs of the family business, especially when project Earth just got started.

But that relationship was interrupted by sin. It's interesting that when I read the verses preceding this one, when the serpent tempted Eve, I envision the story happening much faster. I don't feel like Eve pondered. Did she "weigh in the mind," "think about," or "question?" It very much seems like a quick moving sequence of listen, talk, and respond.

What was God's response to this falling away from His plan? He persisted in His original plan to have a relationship with man. The relationship may have been altered but God desired for the relationship to be restored. Enter the tent of meeting. Enter the tabernacle. Enter the Holy Place. God still desired to be with us, yet sin made a barrier. The relationship lacked the former intimacy we saw in Genesis 3:8. Enter Jesus. He walked among man again. I cannot read the New Testament and envision Jesus in a rush. Just read the story of Lazarus and you can get a pretty good idea of His pace. He stopped to have dinner with people. He stopped to heal people. He stopped to love on children. Yet, the relationship was still limited for He could only be in one place at a time as Jesus in a man's body. Enter the Holy Spirit. Enter the One who would dwell inside of us, teaching us, guiding us, never to leave us again.

And I will ask the Father, and he will give you another Helper to be with you forever, even the Spirit of truth, whom the world cannot receive, because it neither sees him nor knows him. You know him, for he dwells with you and will be in you." (John 14:16–17, ESV)

"But the Advocate, the Holy Spirit, whom the Father will send in my name, will teach you all things and will remind you of everything I have said to you." (John 14: 26, ESV)

This is how you achieve a pondering lifestyle. Let the Holy Spirit, who dwells inside of you teach you about everything you experience. He never sleeps so you can even hear Him during the night. Listen to David, pondering in the night watches. David was a man who sinned greatly, but who loved God greatly. When I read these verses, I feel like God never left his mind.

"By day the LORD directs his love, at night his song is with me— a prayer to the God of my life." (Psalm 42:8, NIV)

"On my bed I remember you; I think of you through the watches of the night." (Psalm 63:6, NIV)

On that note, let me tell you about my pondering roadblock. Someone told me that it would be a great idea to tell the readers about my pondering moments throughout this book. They said it would break up the monotony and suggested a fun title like, 'Pondering Experience 1,984'. She said, 'You know, here's a time where God showed me a little something that I may have pondered in five minutes, or I did not move on for a full 24 hours.' I loved that idea, until I began to search for 'Pondering Experience 1,984' and I could not think of *anything* like that. The more I pondered and searched, the more worried I got. Here I am writing a whole book on pondering and I could not recall *one* single event like she described. After a few weeks of thinking about it off and on, God told me to write this section of the book. He gave me the title before He gave me the details (that happens quite a bit), so, I began my usual routine of sitting with God and writing where He leads. I get a sense when I am supposed to be wrapping up a story and as I felt that was happening in this section, I recalled my friend's suggestion and began to panic. I had *zero* recollections of 'pondering moments,' much less 'Pondering Moment 1,984.' So, I stopped typing and decided to take a bath. I was walking down the hallway to the bathroom, pondering my dilemma. Yes, I pondered my lack of definitive pondering moments. Before I got to the end of the hallway, I realized why I could not recall 'Pondering Moment 1,984.' I do not have 'Pondering Moment 1,984' because pondering is my lifestyle. I dialogue with God all day long. I drive down the street and ponder the things around me from the person on a bicycle to the leaf that blows across my car. I ponder galaxies, atoms, human cells and just about everything in between. Pondering the goodness of God should be as normal as breathing. You do not give one thought to breathing, nor do you tell your lungs to inhale or exhale. Breathing happens because God created it to happen. Pondering as a lifestyle happens when we let the fullness of God that resides in us to radiate out and through everything we encounter.

Just to be clear, pondering can happen in little moments here and there. I probably have had hundreds of those moments, but I guess I never categorized them separately in my mind. To me pondering is one continuous event that gives color and meaning to the tapestry of my life. He is in me, and I am in Him. I don't know how to separate something that God so loving knit together.

I am, therefore, I ponder.

I ponder, therefore I am.

I ponder as a lifestyle.

I ponder the goodness of God.

CONTINUING TO PRACTICE THE PONDER

My deep desire is to ultimately is to lead you to your own personal, intimate interactions with God straight from His word. In this section, I would like to lead you in a short and easy approach to ponder straight from His word.

On the following pages you will find a title that corresponds to the section titles in this book. You will be asked to do a task and then answer a few questions. You can probably go through each activity in one sitting.

Remember, when we ponder, we slow down and give time for the Holy Spirit to speak, for fresh wind to blow on you and for the Word of God to dwell richly within you. Pondering is an art that develops as your love for Him grows and grows. You will *want* to stay longer. You will *want* to sit and be silent. You will *want* more of Him. It is worth the effort as a little time and a little unhurried breathing can usher you into His presence quicker than you realize.

His presence is what we want. His presence brings comfort, peace, wisdom and joy and it silences the shouts of the enemy. The enemy will not roar in His presence. The enemy will not stay in His presence. The enemy will be silent and leave. That is why God's presence is so important. His presence brings what we need. Learn to sit with Him. It is well worth your time. My goal is to bring you to God and His word, so let's begin.

For the LORD is God, and he created the heavens and earth and put everything in place. He made the world to be lived in, not to be a place of empty chaos. "I am the LORD," he says, "and there is no other." Isaiah 45:18 (NLT)

DAY ONE
PEACE

Find a scripture on peace. You can look in the back of your Bible in the index or do an online search for scriptures on peace. Find one that resonates with you, or to say that another way, the scripture just seems to leap off the page, or the scripture seems like it is written just for you. I have included a few scripture references if you should need them.

Scriptures on Peace: Colossians 3:15; Psalms 4:8; Romans 8:6; 2 Thessalonians 3:16. Write out the one that speaks to you below.

_____

_____

_____

_____

_____

_____

SCRIPTURE REFERENCE

Read it again silently or out loud. Write down the first thing in that verse that stands out to you.

_____

_____

_____

_____

Then answer the following questions. You don't have to answer every question. I will give you a few to get you thinking.

- Why would God bring that part of the scripture out to you?

- What area in your life is He speaking to?

- Does this bring you peace? Joy? Excitement?

- What adjustments do you need to make in response to what He showed you?

- What can you praise your heavenly Father for right now?

_____

_____

_____

_____

This is how you ponder. Allow God's word to sit in your mind for longer periods of time. Think about this verse and what He said to you.

Be still.

Breathe.

Ponder.

Do not feel obligated by the space below, but sometimes after pondering I get new thoughts and ideas. Write or creatively express any new revelation or just thank Him specifically for what you learned by pondering *peace*. If nothing else, write *peace* in the space below and do something with each letter like make them thicker or shaded. The goal is just to spend a little more time listening for His voice.

DAY TWO
SURRENDER

Find a scripture on surrender. When looking for scriptures on a specific topic, you can look at the index in the back of your Bible for that word or topic. You can search the internet or ask other people if they have a verse on that word or topic. Even if the actual word 'surrender' does not appear in the verse, you are looking for the essence of the verse to speak on our surrender to Him. Sidenote: the actual word 'surrender' does appear in the Bible, but it is probably talking about surrender in military terms. I am talking about our surrender to God. In case it is difficult to wade through this, I have included a few scripture references. Find one that resonates with you, or to say that another way, the scripture seems to leap off the page or the scripture seems like it is written just for you.

Scriptures on surrender: James 4:7; Romans 6:13; Matthew 11:29; Exodus 19:5-6. Write out the one that speaks to you below.

_____

_____

_____

_____

SCRIPTURE REFERENCE

Read it again silently or out loud. Write down the first thing in that verse that stands out to you.

_____

_____

_____

_____

_____

Then answer the following questions. You do not have to answer every question. I will give you a few to get you thinking.

- Why would God bring that part of the scripture out to you?

- What area in your life is He speaking to?

- Does this bring you peace? Joy? Excitement?

- What adjustments do you need to make in response to what He showed you?

- What can you praise your heavenly Father for right now?

_____

_____

_____

_____

_____

This is how you ponder. Allow God's Word to linger so that you can look at it from different angles. Think about this verse and what He said to you.

Be still.

Breathe.

Ponder.

Do not feel obligated by the space below, but sometimes after pondering I get new thoughts and ideas. Write or creatively express any new revelation or just thank Him specifically for what you learned by pondering *surrender*. Remember, you can even creatively rewrite the word *surrender*.

BREAKTHROUGH

As you have probably noticed, I always begin with "Find a scripture on _____," but as I noted earlier, the specific word you are looking for may not be readily found or it is used in another context like we learned with the word *surrender*. The word *breakthrough* is one of those words that may not appear in many verses, but it is a subject that God loves. Even if the exact word *breakthrough* does not appear in the verse, find a verse that speaks of the way God has provided for our victory. We have been set free by the work of Jesus on the cross. Our enemy wants us to listen to his lies and enslave ourselves to him, for whom we obey becomes our master (Romans 6:16). In case this is not an easy task for you, I have included a few scripture references. Find one that resonates with you, seems to leap off the page, or the scripture seems like it is written just for you.

Scriptures on breakthrough: Isaiah 54:17; Micah 2:13; 2 Corinthians 10:4; 2 Corinthians 9:8. Write it out the one that speaks to you below.

_____

_____

_____

_____

_____

_____

Read it again silently or out loud. Write down the first thing in that verse that stands out to you.

_____

_____

_____

_____

_____

Then answer the following questions. You do not have to answer every question. I will give you a few to get you thinking.

- Why would God bring that part of the scripture out to you?

- What area in your life is He speaking to?

- Does this bring you peace? Joy? Excitement?

- What adjustments do you need to make in response to what He showed you?

- What can you praise your heavenly Father for right now?

_____

_____

_____

_____

This is how you ponder. God's word is so rich that He can bring out new shades of meaning each time you read it when you give Him time. Think about this verse and what He said to you.

Be still.

Breathe.

Ponder.

Do not feel obligated by the space below, but sometimes after pondering I get new thoughts and ideas. Write or creatively express any new revelation or just thank Him specifically for what you learned by pondering *breakthrough*. Remember, you can even creatively rewrite the word *breakthrough* as it just gives space and time to listen for Him.

IDENTITY

I have already noted that there is not always a scripture that has the specific word you are looking for in it. *Identity* is another one of those words that probably does not appear in many verses, but it is a subject that God finds of utmost importance. He has much to say about your identity. Again, when looking for scriptures on a specific topic, you may need the help of others or the internet. Even if the word *identity* does not appear in the verse, the essence of the verse still speaks of your identity in Christ Jesus. Just in case this is not an easy task for you, I have included a few scripture references. Find one that resonates with you, or to say that another way, the scripture just seems to leap off the page, or the scripture seems like it is written just for you.

Scriptures on identity: 1 John 3:1; 1 Peter 2:9; Jeremiah 1.5; Galatians 3:27.

Write it out the one that speaks to you below.

_____

_____

_____

_____

_____

_____

Read it again silently or out loud. Write down the first thing in that verse that stands out to you.

_____

_____

_____

_____

_____

Then answer the following questions. You do not have to answer every question. I will give you a few to get you thinking.

- Why would God bring that part of the scripture out to you?

- What area in your life is He speaking to?

- Does this bring you peace? Joy? Excitement?

- What adjustments do you need to make in response to what He showed you?

- What can you praise your heavenly Father for right now?

_____

_____

_____

_____

This is how you ponder. Even if the scripture is a familiar one, you may be in a new season of your life and something that never stood out to you previously, now resonates with you. Think about this verse and what He said to you.

Be still.

Breathe.

Ponder.

Do not feel obligated by the space below, but sometimes after pondering I get new thoughts and ideas. Write or creatively express any new revelation or just thank Him specifically for what you learned by pondering *identity*. Remember, you can even creatively rewrite the word *identity*.

D A Y   F I V E

HOPE

You may not have to strain to find a scripture on hope, but always remember that just because the actual word is not in the scripture, the essence of the scripture still may speak of the hope that God gives. God is always talking about hope. He is always giving hope. He is our hope. Therefore, you may be able to find quite a few verses on this topic, but continue to use friends, the internet or the index in your Bible, if needed. The goal is to find the scripture that God wants to give you on hope. Again, in case this is not an easy task for you, I have included a few scripture references. Find one that resonates with you, or to say that another way, the scripture just seems to leap off the page, or the scripture seems like it is written just for you.

Scriptures on hope: Philippians 1:6; Romans 15:13; Colossians 1:27; Jeremiah 29:11.

Write out the one that speaks to you below.

_____

_____

_____

_____

SCRIPTURE REFERENCE

Read it again silently or out loud. Write down the first thing in that verse that stands out to you.

_____

_____

_____

_____

_____

Then answer the following questions. You do not have to answer every question. I will give you a few to get you thinking.

- Why would God bring that part of the scripture out to you?

- What area in your life is He speaking to?

- Does this bring you peace? Joy? Excitement?

- What adjustments do you need to make in response to what He showed you?

- Is there a need to praise Him or tell Him of your gratefulness for this revelation?

_____

_____

_____

_____

_____

This is how you ponder. God's word is always relevant so let it soak within you. Think about this verse and what He said to you.

Be still.

Breathe.

Ponder.

Do not feel obligated by the space below, but sometimes after pondering I get new thoughts and ideas. Write or creatively express any new revelation or just thank Him specifically for what you learned by pondering *hope*. Remember, you can even creatively rewrite the word *hope* as it just gives space and time to listen for Him.

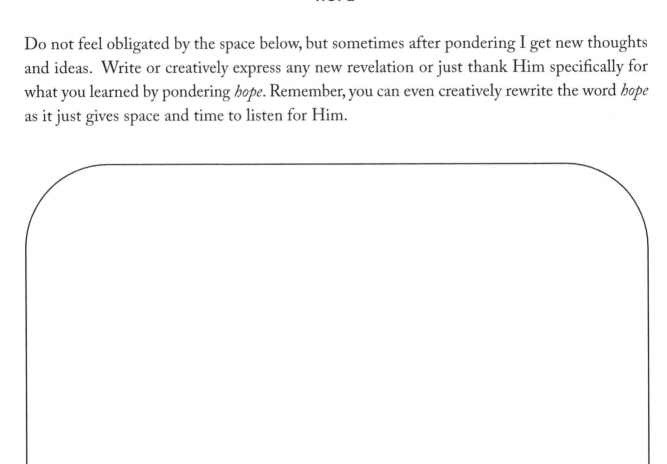

CHANGE

You will find a lot of verses with the word *change,* but they may be referring to an action that someone needs to do instead of what we are looking for, which is the change God wants to bring about in our lives. God desires that we be changed from glory to glory, to be changed in our thought life or to be an agent of change to those around us. He also wants us to have a changed or renewed mind. Change is a subject that God talks about quite often. The internet may be most helpful for this search. A friend may know a verse quite well that talks about the change He is looking for or the change that He is creating in us. In case this is not an easy task for you, I have included a few scripture references. Continue to look for one that resonates with you, or to say that another way, the scripture just seems to leap off the page, or the scripture seems like it is written just for you.

Scriptures on change: Romans 12:2; 2 Corinthians 5:17; 2 Corinthians 3:18; Galatians 2:20. Write out the one that speaks to you below.

_____

_____

_____

_____

SCRIPTURE REFERENCE

Read it again silently or out loud. Write down the first thing in that verse that stands out to you.

_____

_____

_____

_____

_____

Then answer the following questions. You do not have to answer every question. I will give you a few to get you thinking.

- Why would God bring that part of the scripture out to you?

- What area in your life is He speaking to?

- Does this bring you peace? Joy? Excitement?

- What adjustments do you need to make in response to what He showed you?

- What can you praise your heavenly Father for right now?

_____

_____

_____

_____

_____

This is how you ponder. If God's word is always timely, spend time letting Him unwrap it for you. Think about this verse and what He said to you.

Be still.

Breathe.

Ponder.

CHANGE

Do not feel obligated by the space below, but sometimes after pondering I get new thoughts and ideas. Write or creatively express any new revelation or just thank Him specifically for what you learned by pondering *change*. Remember, you can even creatively rewrite the word *change*.

D A Y   S E V E N

GRACE

You may not have to strain to find a scripture on grace. God definitely wants us to know about grace for it is the reason we can have a relationship with Him. His grace is what brought us back into relationship with Him when sin took that away. Grace is the thread that runs from the beginning to the end of our Christian journey and through all of our mistakes in between; therefore, you may be able to find quite a few verses on this amazing grace. Continue to use friends, the internet or the index in your Bible, if needed. The goal is to find the scripture that God wants to give you on grace. I have included a few scripture references. Find one that resonates with you.

Scriptures on grace: Romans 6:14; Ephesians 2:8; James 4:6; 2 Peter 1:2. Write it out the one that speaks to you below.

_____

_____

_____

_____

Scripture reference

Read it again silently or out loud. Write down the first thing in that verse that stands out to you.

_____

_____

_____

_____

Then answer the following questions. You do not have to answer every question. I will give you a few to get you thinking.

- Why would God bring that part of the scripture out to you?

- What area in your life is He speaking to?

- Does this bring you peace? Joy? Excitement?

- What adjustments do you need to make in response to what He showed you?

- What can you praise your heavenly Father for right now?

_____

_____

_____

_____

This is how you ponder. Aren't you thankful that God's word is always speaking to what we need when we need it. Think about this verse and what He said to you.

Be still.

Breathe.

Ponder.

Do not feel obligated by the space below, but sometimes after pondering I get new thoughts and ideas. Write or creatively express any new revelation or just thank Him specifically for what you learned by pondering *grace*. Remember, you can even creatively rewrite the word *grace* as it just gives space and time to listen for Him.

MY "STORY"

I don't have a story, so I guess I don't have a story.

That's the hard part about writing a book. Everyone wants to know your story, but I don't have this huge defining moment when hardship came in so I can tell you that story. I don't have a lifetime of pain from which to draw you in so I can tell you that story. I don't have a story.

Knowing that I am supposed to write a book is nothing new to me, but I didn't know what God wanted me to write about. The feeling grew stronger and stronger as the years went by, and there were times when He would press a little harder into the "write-a-book" feeling, but I did not know what to write about. I don't have a "story."

That "write-a-book" feeling was always in the back of my mind, but that does not help much when all that I had was "writings" with no definitive topic. One day, in frustration, I cried out, "I will write anything You want me to write. Just give me an arrow!" I needed a direction, but I had no "story."

Once, a very seasoned writer called me at the request of a friend trying to help me. She talked for a while about her very successful literary journey, and then asked, "So, what's your book about?" I already knew my answer, but I hesitated. I was hoping a better answer would come to my mind as I swallowed to buy some time. I looked out the window hoping that the answer would appear there. It did not. So, I very softly replied in a tone that easily exposed how I felt about my generic answer, "The goodness of God." I wanted the ground to open up and swallow me. I never felt so subpar in all my life. I knew that she was looking for my "story," but there was no "story." There was just a girl and her God. There was no trauma. There was no pain. There was no abuse. There were no scars. At least not big ones. Nothing to write home about and nothing to write a book about. I had no "story." Our conversation did not last much longer. There wasn't much else to talk about.

So I tucked that book dream away again and returned to normal life. Normal life where God shows up in a whisper, a word, a phrase, a thought in my head, then He downloads a different type of story. A story about His goodness. A story about His grace. A story about all kinds of things, and every one of those stories end the same…in His goodness. The goodness of God; that's a prolific story. We all have those stories. Some are not completed yet; for your journey has just begun, and it's hard to see His goodness in the midst of some of the things life throws your way. Some stories have already been written. I fall in love with those stories where the hardest of hard comes along, or the life that was full of tragedy and pain unspeakable, and the goodness of God won out. As always, those stories give us hope that in the unimaginable pain and hardship, God is still pursuing His children, rescuing the lost and the abandoned and wiping off the dirt. Yes, that is the God I love and the God I serve. But that is not my "story."

My story is filled with love and joy, a little bit of pain and sorrow, but nothing to write home about. Nothing to write a book about. So, I didn't write that book. Instead, I wrote a book about a girl and her really good God. That is my story. My story has only one tragic flaw. The waywardness of me.

I met with a literary coach, and she began to ask questions during our first video meeting. I told her of the vast number of "writings" that I currently had but I had no clear direction for a book. I told her that I was not floundering trying to come up with material, for I had way more than I knew what to do with, but I was floundering in a direction for all of the writings.

I told her the exact amount of these writings and then I said, "I just don't know what to do with all of them, but I don't want to write a book of Vonda's ramblings." She pressed further, "What do you write about?" My heart sunk. I decided to have a more confident approach to that question this time; but when I spoke, I lost my confidence and mumbled, "about how good God is." She peered up from her glasses at me. I assume she was wanting to see if I was in mid-sentence or at least in mid-thought. I was not. But I quickly became mid-thought because I could see that I needed someone to believe in me. I feel that I write good material, I just don't have a "story." So, I began to ramble, "Life is hard. And…I know people say this all the time, but God is good. And…".

I stopped. I turned to stare out of the window. I did not know why answering that question is so hard. God is good, and I want people to know that, but I don't have a "story." She pressed in with more questions to help her understand who I was writing to and why I was writing. I rambled some more. Finally, she asked something like, "What made you begin to see the goodness of God? What happened?" She was digging deeper in search of my "story." I looked away. I sat silently staring out the window again. I had no "story." As I continued to sit there, I felt my dreams fading. I had no hope to write a book. Who would buy it? It is just ramblings on the goodness of God. You could pick up your Bible and read that, I thought in my discouraged moment. My mind quickly ran over my writings. What else was in there besides the goodness of God because obviously everyone was looking for more? Not that God needs more justification to be good, but why would someone pick up my book? I was still staring out the window, thinking of what compels me to write and running my mental eyes over my writings and then I decided that I would just start talking. I needed someone to believe in me.

"I have messed up in life because of poor choices. I have gone my own way. I have made my own decisions and suffered the consequences of that independence, and God still loves me. He still chooses to be abundantly good when I'm not. And so many people think that they are not good enough, and…that's just not true. And I talk to so many people who don't understand how much He loves them and…I don't know. I just write about that so people know. People beat themselves up when God really loves them. They just don't believe it."

I trailed off in my zeal for the love of people and the love of God realizing that I didn't have a "story." I had been looking out the window most of the time while I was talking so I turned to look at her and kind of shrugged my shoulders and looked back out the window. Someone else joined our video meeting so I looked back at the screen. I could see the literary coach smiling. I think I must have apologized or mumbled something about trying to think of something else to say, and she said, 'I got it. I finally heard it.' I just stared at her. I had just finished rambling and said to myself, "she heard it"? She heard what? I began a quick mental replay of what I said. It felt just as bad when reviewing the ramblings as it did when saying them, but somewhere in my mental review, I realized that between what she heard and the new tone in my voice, she found my passion, she found my "arrow."

I found my *arrow*.

I found my *story*.

I have a deep compassion for those who feel less than. I have a deep compassion for those who feel unworthy. I have a deep compassion for those who mess up on the daily and don't have a "story" to blame it on because I am one of those people. I am a girl who trudged through life making choices independent of her heavenly Father and although none of them ended in addictions, trauma, and life-long pain, my "story" is still full of heartache and disappointment, guilt and shame, and the marring of God's name. And that grieves me. And He still loves me. That bewilders me. That floors me. That undoes me. And that is why I write. That is my "story." I am a product of poor choices, yet I still look like a piece of unchipped porcelain; but sin mars us even if it doesn't stick out like a sore thumb. My sin marred me. My sin grieved me. My sin broke His heart. My sin is still sin, and although it does not look like those books that everyone is talking about and everyone is getting healing from, His grace always makes a "story." My "story" looks oh so different, but my "story" is oh so amazing, and oh so full of the same grace.

This book is for you if you regret your poor choices.

This book is for you if you know you could have done better.

This book is for you if you feel less than because you have a good life, but you still have regrets.

This book is for you if you need to know that you may have made a lifetime of small poor choices, but there is hope.

This book is for you if you strive for perfection and have ever regretfully said something like, "I did the best I could, and it turned out okay."

This book is for you if you feel just average and your struggle is nothing to write home about. I wrote about it and all my "writings" ended in the same place…the goodness of God. No matter how fickle my devotion to Him, no matter how many times I failed Him, no matter how many times I left Him out, the goodness of my God always wins.

There is a "story" in these pages. It is a story of hope. It is a story of a good, good Father. It is a story told many times over, of the frailty of man and the love of God. And know this, your "story" is your "story." It doesn't have to look a certain way or have a certain element. It is your "story" and the most important thing about it is to share it. Someone in your sphere of influence needs to hear *your* "story," that's why God put you there.

Don't wait for an "arrow" to tell your "story." I actually didn't wait to share my story. I went years without knowing what to write about for a book, but I constantly wrote about what He was showing me in each season of my life, and I shared those stories with my friends.

You may not be a writer. You may be a talker. Then tell your "story." The most important thing for me was my compassion for people. People need hope. People need a word (Thanks Dad for telling me that).

People have *you* in their life and they need to hear *your* "story." You may not feel that you have a "story," but you do. The writings in this book are a compilation of my ponderings with God. They don't have an arrow in and of themselves, besides the goodness of God, but that is the thread that keeps hope alive and that is the most important part of my story.

I have prayed that you will have fallen more deeply in love with pondering after reading this book. I have prayed that you would be blessed when you took the time to spend unhurried time with your Father. Now share what He has shown you. No, you do not have to write a book. No, you do not have to tell your whole life story. Just share what He showed you today. That's called a story.

You are called to declare His goodness.

> *"I will exalt you, my God and King, and praise your name forever and ever. I will praise you every day; yes, I will praise you forever.*
>
> *Great is the LORD! He is most worthy of praise! No one can measure his greatness.*
>
> *Let each generation tell its children of your mighty acts; let them proclaim your power.*
>
> *I will meditate on your majestic, glorious splendor and your wonderful miracles.*
>
> *Your awe-inspiring deeds will be on every tongue; I will proclaim your greatness.*
>
> *Everyone will share the story of your wonderful goodness; they will sing with joy about your righteousness." Psalm 145:1-7 (NLT)*

Be blessed and happy pondering!

Vonda

ENDNOTES

Below are the names of the referenced content that has been cited in the book. The author does not own the rights to the cited information. Please refer to these endnotes if you'd like more information.

WEEK THREE:

1. Howarth, Helen; "Turn Your Eyes Upon Jesus."

2. Perkus, Benjamin; PhD., founder of The Aroma Freedom Technique.

WEEK SEVEN:

3. Arthur, Kay; author, and speaker.

WEEK EIGHT:

4. Brewer, David; First Baptist Church of Westlake, Louisiana.

WEEK ELEVEN:

5. Bible Hub, https://biblehub.com/commentaries/psalms/84-6.htm

6. Bible Hub, https://biblehub.com/commentaries/psalms/84-6.htm

WEEK FOURTEEN:

7. Powell, Justis'; author.

WEEK TWENTY:

8. McEntire, Wayne; First Baptist Church of Westlake, Louisiana.